FRONTING ONLYS

FRONTING ONLYS

My 2½ Cents Worth of Henry David Thoreau
(as adjusted for inflation, taxes, and mishandling fees)

Tom Beattie

First edition

ISBN-13: 978-0-578-19761-6

whatdoesitprofit press, LLC
P.O. Box 41475
Providence, RI 02904

FOR

David

WITH LOVE

"I went to the woods because I wished to live deliberately, to front only the essential facts of life, and see if I could not learn what it had to teach, and not, when I came to die, discover that I had not lived."

--HENRY DAVID THOREAU, *WALDEN*

INTERVIEW WITH A WOODCHUCK

"Thoreau"?

Yeah, I knew him.

We were neighbors those few years he lived in a cabin by the pond.

(Always wondered how he got a building permit.)

Quiet fella.

Kept to himself mostly.

Walked a lot hereabouts, day and night, rain or shine.

But he'd also sometimes sit for hours stretched out in his doorway. Thinking? Dreaming? Working on his tan? Your guess is as good as mine.

And what a tree hugger! Seen it myself, numerous times. Maple, oak, sycamore--made absolutely no difference to him. Loved birds, fish, and bugs, too. Okay, none of my business. It takes all kinds.

What can I add...? Very tidy, didn't throw wild parties, was big into recycling. Played the flute, recited Homer, sang as he hoed in his bean-field.

Nice guy.

Right?

So imagine my surprise when he killed and ate my brother.

WTF!

Sure, he was arrested and held overnight, but he was released without a hearing, and that, come to find out, was for another completely unrelated crime.

(Shoulda known it was nuts to hope for justice.)

That's all I got.

HENRY DAVID THOREAU

1817 - 1862.

American.

Author, historian, and philosopher.

Naturalist, abolitionist, and social reformer.

Leech, deadbeat, and anarchist?

Well…

Wrote *Walden; or, Life in the Woods.*

Friend of Emerson, Hawthorne, and the Alcott's.

HENRY DAVID THOREAU

(AGE 39)

Benjamin D. Maxham
1856
Ninth-plate daguerreotype

National Portrait Gallery
Smithsonian Institution
Gift of anonymous donor

Hero to grassrooters and rebooters, right and left.

Inspired Tolstoy, Proust, and Hemingway.

Among others.

Including me.

T-SHIRTABLE

In the 1960's, the late, great Walter Harding published a benchmark biography of Thoreau, which, I confess, I've consulted frequently in writing this my own wannabe work. Harding lamented that the "man on the street" back then knew only that Thoreau had lived at Walden Pond and spent some time in jail. I doubt that many on my street now, man or woman, know that much! Yours either.

My own unscientific survey suggests that most people today remember Thoreau for one truly t-shirtable quote, even if some don't remember it was he who said it:

"If a man does not keep pace with his companions, perhaps it is because he hears a different drummer. Let him step to the music which he hears, however measured or far away."

(I'll take an X-large in teal, please!)

But all that changes now.

I propose to write an ode to reflection. My theme: Who was Henry David Thoreau and why should anybody still give a damn? Part American Lit, part retrofit! And since I consider myself more anybody than anybody, there'll be plenty of me thrown in, too, just to keep things interesting.

PLEASE HOLD ALL APPLAUSE UNTIL THE END

"I should not talk so much about myself if there were anybody else whom I knew as well."

--HENRY DAVID THOREAU, *WALDEN*

DON'T!

I first came under Thoreau's influence in high school in 1973. I'd picked up a copy of *Walden* at Waldenbooks. (Go figure!) It wasn't on the recommended reading list, but it was a Signet Classic and that was recommendation enough for me. I finished it in a day and a half, cutting classes and skipping extracurriculars. I was a good student and a first-time offender, so I didn't get into serious trouble for going AWOL, but a counselor did give me a Thoreau advisory: "Don't be fooled by that flower-power freak, kid! You'll end up a loser. Or worse. Understand? You've got brains. Use them. Make something of your life!"

(Do I *have* to?)

As readers of my growing-up-gay memoir *Ad Majorem* will recall, it was in high school that I first began to realize I liked men even more than Signet Classics. And I had brains enough to understand that as a homosexual in those days I'd be able to make something of my life only if I could manage to fool everybody. I knew next to nothing in theory or practice about man-man attraction, but I knew being thus-thus attracted meant, in theory and practice, I'd be regarded as next to nothing.

It seemed that mine was to be a life of the quietest desperation.

Hmph.

Enter Henry David Thoreau…

HOW MANY A MAN

"How many a man has dated a new era of his life from the reading of a book!"
--HENRY DAVID THOREAU, *WALDEN*

SATURDAY'S CHILD

Thoreau was born on July 12th, 1817, a Saturday. His birthplace, his mom's family farmhouse in Concord,

Massachusetts, still stands and has been turned into a cool museum.

Thoreau was named David Henry, but he would switch that around to Henry David as an adult, if unofficially.

The old nursery rhyme warns that Saturday's child must work for a living. I don't know if that's based on actual Sat. stats, but it was true in Thoreau's case. Of course, Thoreau would radically re-define "work" and "living" in the process...

NO SWEAT

"It is not necessary that a man should earn his living by the sweat of his brow, unless he sweats easier than I do."
--HENRY DAVID THOREAU, *WALDEN*

SATURDAY'S CHILD II

Coincidentally, I'm a Saturday's child, too!

Sorta.

I was born at midnight one Friday-going-on-Saturday sixty years ago in Providence, Rhode Island. My mom's doctor let her choose which day would be recorded as my D.O.B. With characteristic common sense, Mom said, so she always said, "It must be that which is just *beginning*, no?"

Yes!

So Saturday it was.

And I immediately got dressed in my work clothes.

As a Friday's child I would've been loving and giving, but...

Always a day late and a dollar short.

WHO WAS IN CHARGE OF SENDING OUT INVITATIONS?

My husband David and I took a drive to Concord on July 12th, 2017, the 200th anniversary of Thoreau's birth. We'd been before, but we wanted to be there on that special day, and since we live only about an hour away, well, what the hay!

I expected hordes, but David and I constituted a majority of two at most of the Thoreau sites.

Sheesh.

A reporter from a Boston radio station, frantic for a few sound bites from, ahem, anybody, asked me about my "relationship" with Thoreau.

THOREAU'S BIRTHPLACE

Thoreau Farm
341 Virginia Road
Concord, MA

www.thoreaufarm.org

"'*Relationship*'?!!! Why? What've you heard? Okay, fine, he's my secret boyfriend, but don't tell my Lawfully Wedded, at least not until after the festivities. I wouldn't want to cause a scene--or miss out on the cake."

BREAKING NEWS:
Thoreau's Sordid Love Shack Exposed!

(Only joking.)

No, I mumbled something nothing-much into the mic, "an historic day," blah blah blah, making it very unlikely that I'll ever get my own talk show.

David and I toured the Thoreau birthplace (just us), viewed the Thoreau exhibit at the Concord Museum (ditto), and stopped by Thoreau's grave to lay a bouquet of flowers (ditto ditto).

Where *was* everybody?

Crowding into the Main Streets Café!

David and I joined the village people there for a delicious lupper, then headed home.

Can't wait for the 300th!

INTERVIEW WITH A TOWN CLERK

"Thoreau"?

18

No, sorry, I don't have a "Henry David" in my files, only a "David Henry."

That your guy?

Well, if so, you tell him to get his ass into this office a.s.a.p.

He's got *paperwork* to do!

You gotta change ya name to change ya name.

Who doesn't know that!

I oughta report him to the DMV.

EARLY ON

Thoreau's father had a small pencil-making business, one of our nation's first.

"Thoreau's Improved Drawing Pencils, for the Nicest Uses of the Drawing Master, Surveyor, Engineer, Architect, and Artist generally."

Company profits, unfortunately, early on, anyway, barely kept Dad, Mom, and their four kids out of poverty.

Thoreau was third in a symmetrical girl-boy-boy-girl series.

Which, as most of us latter-halfs can attest, usually means hand-me-downs and lots of waiting arounds for our turn at whatever.

Youth appears to have been a happy period in Thoreau's life. Kittens, kites, custards, swimming in summer, sledding in winter, learning to read and reading, learning to write and writing...

Not to mention frequent visits from eccentric relatives.

The Thoreau's were of French-Canadian descent.

Which, if my own F-C descendancy is typical, equals one large, extended family.

We invented them!

Hearts of gold, without exception, but if the truth be told, according to mold, yeah, eccentric.

(Don't get me started!)

As a kid, Thoreau was afraid of thunder, survived his share of cuts and bruises, and believed in Santa Claus until a snot-nosed girl in his class told him that his parents had stuffed his Christmas stocking with candy they'd bought at her father's store. In my own formative years, I likewise was "a-scared" of storms, spent many an accidental hour in the ER, and believed in Santa until I read that spoiler about Thoreau's Christmas candy.

(Thanks, Snot Nose!)

HIGHER ED

By the time Thoreau was sixteen, his father's pencil start-up had started up, and the family's finances had improved. There was enough money to send Thoreau off to Harvard.

Thoreau's program of studies was what we would call liberal arts. Greek and Latin, literature, history, philosophy, theology, some science. It was the kind of generalist education that today is generally frowned upon. Getting a good job after graduation is the name of the game now, so students have had to become more pragmatic, plotting, and projecting. The title of a song from the hit Broadway musical *Avenue Q* sums up the current sentiment: "What Do You Do with a B.A. in English?"

Indeed.

As a B.A. in English, I can only tell you what I did. I found ways to make myself useful to all the people with good jobs who couldn't staple two words together because they hadn't learned how to do so in college! I wrote letters, brochures, and grant proposals. I freelanced, interned, and entry-leveled. I consulted, contracted, and, yes, generalized.

And I've never questioned my liberal arts education.

Not even when I went to see *Avenue Q*.

(Silly puppets.)

ON TRACK

"Every path but your own is the path of fate. Keep on your own track, then."

--HENRY DAVID THOREAU, *WALDEN*

TAKE THIS JOB AND...

Fresh out of Harvard in 1837, Thoreau returned to Concord and found employment as a teacher.

That didn't last long!

The authorities wanted Thoreau to beat his students with a stick when they misbehaved, as was accepted practice. Problem was, Thoreau disapproved of such methods. When ordered to toughen-up-or-else, he gave some random beatings, deserved and not, then resigned his position. One of the random undeserved's vowed that when he grew up he would get even, but when he grew up he vowed that Thoreau was the kindest man he'd ever known, and forgot all about revenge.

("Don't be fooled by that flower-power freak, kid!")

A BETTER WAY

In 1838, Thoreau and his older brother John, another disillusioned teacher, decided to start their own school.

(If you can't beat 'em…?)

Their "Concord Academy" was progressive. Classroom learning was augmented by field trips, walkabouts, and show-and-tell's. Order was a point of honor--the young scholars had to promise to behave, then were taught the importance of keeping their promises.

Among the little women and little men who would be enrolled as students was six-year-old Louisa May Alcott (*Little Women* and *Little Men*.)

The effort was a success, but when brother John got sick and died suddenly in 1842, brother Henry couldn't go it alone.

"We regret to announce…"

The school closed.

WORK-LIFE BALANCE

Thoreau was one of those smart people who don't fit into the professional world.

(Too smart to want to?)

And, of course, he didn't have my counselor to set him straight.

(No pun intended.)

For Thoreau, it was a matter of work-life balance.

He inclined to a simple lifestyle because it allowed him to work less and live more--

"Many a forenoon have I stolen away [row-boating], preferring to spend thus the most valued part of the day; for I was rich, if not in money, in sunny hours and summer days, and spent them lavishly; nor do I regret that I did not waste more of them in the workshop or the teacher's desk."

In my "day job" as an HR manager, I've seen this same spirit in the younger generation. They seem to think and care more than us older cogs ever did about how the daily grind will impact their health, their relationships, even their activities, hobbies, and bucket lists.

Flex-time, job sharing, telecommuting.

Sooo Thoreau!

(Me? I recently took a day off from my HR duties to work at home on this book, and I felt guilty as hell.)

PRICE CHECK

"[T]he cost of a thing is the amount of what I will call life which is required to be exchanged for it."

--HENRY DAVID THOREAU, *WALDEN*

GAPS IN EMPLOYMENT

No, Thoreau wasn't the 9-to-5 type. He sometimes worked a regular shift making pencils for his dad, but he was reluctant to join the family business on a permanent basis.

Luckily, though, Thoreau could always temp-labor for ready cash. Harvesting crops, mending fences, and handyman-ing around town.

Eventually, Thoreau settled into the role of caretaker for Concord's resident sage Ralph Waldo Emerson.

It would prove to be a savvy career move.

INTERVIEW WITH A PRODUCTION MANAGER

"Thoreau"?

You must mean the boss's kid.

Yeah, he worked here in the pencil factory--*briefly*!

Smart little bastard, too, I must say. Figured out ways to improve our methods. Added clay to the graphite to make it stronger.

(Who knew!)

That boy had one hell of a future in writing instruments.

But then he up and quits without so much as a week's notice. Said he'd made a perfect #2 and that was enough for him.

Tell it to Quality Control!

CAPTAIN HOBGOBLIN

Getting back to Emerson...

Who?

"A foolish consistency is the hobgoblin of little minds."

Oh, him!

Emerson was an American intellectual celebrity, a former preacher turned essayist and lecturer.

Many of his ideas have taken root in our national consciousness.

Self-reliance.
Self-determination.
Self-actualization.

"What lies behind us and what lies before us are tiny matters compared to what lies within us."

26

(Too bad fridge magnets hadn't been invented yet!)

Emerson was to become Thoreau's mentor, encouraging him to write, giving him pointers, and introducing him to other authors and important people in publishing.

He was quick to recognize Thoreau's potential.

But Emerson would remain always first, Thoreau second, at best, in popular opinion. To many contemporaries, Thoreau was an imitator, a parrot. And that relative ranking persisted long after Thoreau's death.

"A foolish consistency is the hobgoblin of little minds."

I'LL TRADE YOU TWO EMERSON'S

In 2009, Topps put out a Thoreau trading card as part of its American Heritage Series. You probably can still get one on eBay for $2 or less.

The card includes a trivia question: Who was Thoreau's Walden Pond landlord?

Answer: Ralph Waldo Emerson.

True.

But why did Thoreau have to share his card with RWE!

Geez.

INTERVIEW WITH A VILLAGE GOSSIP

"Thoreau"?

Sure, I knew him, and all about him.

He was an admirer of Ralph Waldo Emerson.

The *writer.*

Concord's own!

Who could forget his genius--

"A fuelish viscosity is a sign of bad wine."

Brilliant!

What's that you say, "Thoreau wrote, too"?

News to me!

* * *

PLAY THE HOBGOBLIN HOME GAME!

It's my idiosyncrasy to punk Em's famous line,
e.g., *"Lights on a ficus tree are a bitch to unwind,"*
or *"A bride with a registry avoids a two toaster bind ,"*
or even *"Washington D.C. is full of horses' behinds."*
Try it and tell me if you're similarly inclined!

28

THE TRANSCENDENTALISTS

In the 1840's, Emerson and his back-up band of Bay State brainiacs, including alleged lip-syncer Thoreau, burst onto the scene as the Transcendentalists.

It was a very granular group.

Their Greatest Hits?

The Transcendentalists taught that we humans are naturally good, that we are part of a natural world, and that we ought to rely more on our natural instincts, intuitions, and insights. They believed that everything is related, sacred, and originally pure. They elevated the individual, celebrated the "I", and consecrated the "eye." They sought the cause in the effect, the hiding in the hidden, and the past, present, and future in the now.

They were spiritual-but-not-religious long before that was a thing.

Upcoming tour dates to be announced.

Like them on Facebook.

IS THIS IOWA?

"Heaven is under our feet as well as over our heads."
--HENRY DAVID THOREAU, *WALDEN*

29

WALDEN

Ladies and gentlemen:
Please take a moment to silence your cell phones as
our feature presentation is about to begin.

(Finally!)

THEME MUSIC plays under OPENING CREDITS.

WALDEN
Or, Life in the Woods.
Based on a true story.

FOLLOWED BY -- CLOSE UP -- WOODCHUCK #1.

VOICE OVER.
"How much wood would a woodchuck chuck if a
woodchuck could... Hey, who's that hairy *homo sapien*
over there digging with a shovel?"

PAN TO: THOREAU.

(Can you believe I've never studied screenwriting?)

Walden is Thoreau's masterpiece, a chronicle of two-
plus years in his life, July 4th, 1845, to September 6th,
1847, to be precise.

As Thoreau himself reports--

"...I lived alone, in the woods, a mile from any neighbor,
in a house which I had built myself, on the shore of
Walden Pond in Concord, Massachusetts..."

WALDEN;

OR,

LIFE IN THE WOODS.

By HENRY D. THOREAU,
AUTHOR OF "A WEEK ON THE CONCORD AND MERRIMACK RIVERS."

I do not propose to write an ode to dejection, but to brag as lustily as chanticleer in the
morning, standing on his roost, if only to wake my neighbors up. — Page 92.

BOSTON:
TICKNOR AND FIELDS.
M DCCC LIV.

WALDEN

Title Page
First Edition
Published by Ticknor and Fields
Boston
1854

Library of Congress

Growing much of his own food, dressing down, kicking around…

Simplifying, why?-ing...

Fronting only the essentials, necessaries, and needful's.

Thoreau considered his time at Walden an experiment, his aim, in part, to prove that it's crazy to let crazy stuff drive us crazy--

"Why should we live with such hurry and waste of life?"

(Didn't I just say that, T?)

MARROW

"I wanted to live deep and suck out all the marrow of life, to live so sturdily and Spartan-like as to put to rout all that was not life."

--HENRY DAVID THOREAU, *WALDEN*

OPEN CONCEPT

There's an interesting show on HGTV about people shopping for "tiny" houses. Most of them are young pups wanting to sit out the property and possessions procession, but every now and again there's an older and wiser down-sizer.

The tiny houses are, wait for it, tiny--500 square feet or less. Typical loft bedrooms are usually short on headroom, and the baths rarely have tubs. Countertops are frequently not much larger than school cafeteria trays, and closets no bigger than student lockers. Anything "oversized" *is*!

Thoreau's cabin at Walden Pond was *very* tiny, the tiniest, well under the HGTV max. Ten feet wide by fifteen feet long. That'd be 150 squares. A nitpicker might note that there was also a root cellar beneath and a small garret above, but those wouldn't have added much usable space. Today, by way of comparison, a standard garden shed, carport, or self-storage unit is at least 10 x 15.

Thoreau's cabin had a door (in front), two windows (one on either side), and a fireplace (in the rear). The structure was shingled without and plastered within.

The interior was "open concept"--

"All the attractions of a house were concentrated in one room; it was kitchen, chamber, parlor, and keeping-room."

No water, electricity, or other utilities, of course. No carpeting or curtains, either, in case you were wondering.

Some of Thoreau's furnishings have survived and are on display at the Concord Museum. A bed, a desk, a chair. Small. Primitive. Unadorned.

And very uncomfortable.

(You can take my word for it. I once sample-sat at a replica of Thoreau's desk. Not a happy ergonomic memory!)

Thoreau also had a table, two more chairs, a looking-glass, a wash bowl, a lamp, and a set of tongs and andirons. He'd jettisoned three limestone paperweights because they were too high maintenance--

"I was terrified to find that they required to be dusted daily,... and threw them out the window in disgust."

For cooking/eating Thoreau had a few pots and pans, a kettle, a dipper, a jug for oil, a jug for molasses, three plates, one cup, two knives, two forks, and one spoon.

(You can usually find more than that soaking in my sink at any given time.)

Thoreau was an advocate of utility in man-made things, and he disliked and distrusted ornamentation. Many of today's tiny-housers, if those on HGTV are representative, likewise live for utility. Their vocabularies consist of one word: "multi-functional." But they won't compromise on style! They want character, they want charm, they want fancy finishes! Barrel ceilings, pocket doors, shiplap...

"Are those real Venetian tiles on your backsplash?"

"Yes!"

"What, BOTH of them?!!!"

34

10 X 15

"My dwelling was small.... I could hardly entertain an echo in it."
--HENRY DAVID THOREAU, *WALDEN*

(My, that *was* small, small, small!)

PUTTING IT TOGETHER

In *Walden*, Thoreau gives a detailed account of his cabin project. What he used for materials, where he sourced them, and what they cost. What he did, when and how he did it, and what resulted. What he learned, what he would teach others, and what it all meant.

Thoreau's total construction expenses came to $28.12½.

(They had half-cent coins then.)

Most of his cash went for supplies, a little for transport of same. Thoreau economized by appropriating some wood, stone, and sand from the building site. He had to buy a lathe and borrow an ax, but apparently already owned whatever other tools were required. He had some volunteered help in framing (including Emerson), but he did the rest of the work himself, so factor in something for sweat equity.

Thoreau had a knack for reclaiming and reusing. His windows weren't new, nor were most of his fireplace and chimney bricks. And much of his lumber and some of his hardware came from another *petite maison* he'd purchased and taken apart board by board!

COST-BENEFIT ANALYSIS

"I intend to build me a house which will surpass any on the main street in Concord in grandeur and luxury, as soon as it pleases me as much and will cost me no more than my present one."

--HENRY DAVID THOREAU, *WALDEN*

INSERT PICTURE

The first edition of *Walden* had an illustration of Thoreau's cabin that was based on a sketch by his younger sister Sophia.

(See repro on page 31.)

Thoreau himself approved of the rendering, although he thought Sis had made the peak of the roof too high and didn't get some of the trees quite right.

Other than that, beeeautiful.

"Thanks a mil, Sophs!"

"You're welcome--I think."

INTERVIEW WITH A DEVELOPER

"Thoreau"?

No, sorry, I don't think I ever met him.

But then I don't socialize much. Too busy flipping houses.
There's lots of junk out there with my name on it!

Right now I'm working on a "tiny" out by the pond.

(At first, I thought it was a Port-A-John.)

But I'll make something of it. Wait and see if I don't!
Brand new master suite; spacious, fully-applianced kitchen;
maybe even a media center.

The dump's worthless now, but you know what they say--

Location! Location! Location!

$28.12½

What kind of a place can you build for $28.12½ today?

That sum won't get you much more than a couple of
2 x 4's and a handful of nails.

(I've tried.)

So…

Instead of feet, think inches; instead of Lowe's, think Michaels.

Sometime near the end of May 2017, I made a scale model of Thoreau's cabin.

(See photo on opposite page.)

My expenses were as follows:

Foam board (3 sheets @ $7.49 ea.)	*$22.47*
Masking tape (1 roll)	*$3.79*
Supplies subtotal	*$26.26*
RI sales tax (7%)	*$1.84*
Total $$$ spent	*$28.10*

Thoreau didn't have to pay sales tax, but I did and I did. He included transportation costs in his tally, as you will recall, but I combined my shopping with routine errands and thus didn't incur any delivery fees. I used my own tools, as had Thoreau, although in place of ax, handsaw, and hammer, I substituted X-acto knife, scissors, and glue stick.

No, my cabin doesn't have a working door, windows, or fireplace, but…

I still have 2½ cents left over for improvements!!!

MY CABIN

Built 2017

10" x 15"

0 Bedrooms
0 Baths

(Currently off market)

I wanted to make my cabin out of balsa wood, it being both natural and renewable, but that would've been too expensive. I'd rejected pipe cleaners, clay, and papier-mâché, although all within budget, because they lacked character, allowing themselves to be manipulated too easily. I'd considered popsicle sticks, too, both cheap and readily available, but I didn't have the heart to deny them their destiny. No, I could not be so crafty a crafter.

Overall, foam board served me well. It was strong enough to stand up for itself without much urging on my part. A little tape to join and seal up seams was all that was required. Yes, it yielded a few rough edges, but those were my fault and failing. I was digitally compromised, fearful at first of slicing a finger. A timid man seldom cuts cleanly, no matter how honorable his purpose. I did improve with practice, however. My chimney, which was pieced together last, is by far the soundest element.

Granted, foam board is a plastic product that's slow to biodegrade, so environmentalists may scoff. To them I would say this: I've got an X-acto knife and now know how to use it. Have you never ordered takeaway in Styrofoam containers? Let us learn from our scraps as we do from our scrapes.

(Translation: Gimme a break!)

I intend to make an even grander and more luxurious cabin model as soon as it pleases me as much and Michaels has a 50% off coupon in the newspaper.

IF YOU BUILD IT...

Of course, wild apples to wild apples, Thoreau's
$28.12½ would equate to approximately $1000 today.

Some people claim online that it's still possible to
reproduce Thoreau's cabin exactly as-was for a thou. I
don't know enough about construction to be able to
confirm or deny, but they couldn't say that on the
internet if it weren't true, right?

I think I know enough about people, however, to be able
to guess that few if any of those onliners are actually
living in their reproduced cabins.

*"OMG, it's great! We use it for storing bicycles, hosting
tiki parties, and hiding holiday presents. And when
Junior throws a Transcendental tantrum, we send him to
the cabin for time-out."*

ATTACH PART A TO PART B,
BEING CAREFUL NOT TO...

And there's a company in Massachusetts that will sell
you a Thoreau cabin kit, complete with blueprints, step-
by-step's, and all the materials you will need,
appropriately sized, pre-cut, and labeled.

Yours for only $22,400.

(What are you waiting for?)

"Hello, Customer Support? Sorry, but I'd like to exchange the Thoreau cabin kit you sent me. No, my mistake. I ordered the wrong item! I wanted one of your House of the Seven Gables snap-together's. I hear they're wicked easy to assemble."

FOR THE BIRDS

"There is some of the same fitness in a man's building his own house that there is in a bird's building its own nest. Who knows but if men constructed their dwellings with their own hands, and provided food for themselves and families simply and honestly enough, the poetic faculty would be universally developed, as birds universally sing when they are so engaged?"

--HENRY DAVID THOREAU, *WALDEN*

YUMMY!

What did Thoreau eat at Walden?

By his own report: bread, rice, beans, potatoes, peas, corn, apples, pumpkin, watermelon, and pork.

(No Twinkies?)

Thoreau really enjoyed baking his daily bread. His was an unleavened loaf made of rye and coarse meal mixed with salt and water and warmed before an open fire.

He'd adapted a recipe found in the writings of Marcus Porcius Cato, an ancient Roman who obviously never watched the Food Network.

Incidentally, some credit Thoreau with inventing raisin bread at Walden as a variation on Cato...

(Thoreau's Test Kitchen!)

During the writing of this book, I tried the Thoreau Diet for three days. I ate only what might've been served up by Thoreau himself had I been invited over for dinner.

Okay, my bread was store-bought, my rice microwavable, and my peas and corn canned, but my apples and watermelon were re-enactment perfect.

(I passed on the potatoes, pumpkin, and pork.)

Overall, it was satisfying.

But borrrrrring!

HOW MUCH?!!!

"My food alone cost me in money about twenty-seven cents a week."
--HENRY DAVID THOREAU, *WALDEN*

("Stock up at A&P when there's a sale on pork rind!")

PURSLANE

Thoreau states in *Walden* that he once made a meal out of a dish of purslane, boiled and salted.

In case you don't know, purslane is a weed.

Some would tell you otherwise, but they'd be wrong.

I recently grew some for laughs from seeds in a pot.

(See photo on opposite page.)

I didn't win any ribbons at the Rhode Island State Fair, but I did harvest enough of the rubbery sprouts to be able to try a small dish, boiled and salted.

Yuck!

And I usually *love* green food.

Pears, pickles, pistachio ice cream...

There are recipes for purslane soup, spreads, and smoothies, but I think I'll always prefer mine in other people's bellies.

There ain't enough Ranch dressing in the world...

It's a *weed.*

(And don't get all P.C. on me.)

MY PURSLANE

Summer 2017

(Don't strain your eyes!)

A GOOD SOURCE OF IRON

"There is a certain class of unbelievers who sometimes ask me such questions as, if I think I can live on vegetable food alone; ...I am accustomed to answer such, that I can live on board nails."
--HENRY DAVID THOREAU, *WALDEN*

(Not surprised!)

WHATEVER MY OWN PRACTICE

Thoreau was a vegetarian *in principle.*

Which meant he ate meat.

Fish, fowl, and a variety of other animals, including, yes, a woodchuck that once raided his bean-field.

But Thoreau wasn't always proud of his menu choices.

Meat gave him spiritual *agida.*

As he confesses in *Walden*--

"Whatever my own practice may be, I have no doubt that it is a part of the destiny of the human race, in its gradual improvement, to leave off eating animals, as surely as the savage tribes have left off eating each other when they came in contact with the more civilised."

As a Transcendentalist, Thoreau felt a common bond
with other creatures, and devouring any of them was bad
manners--

"Is it not a reproach that man is a carnivorous animal?
True, he can and does live, in a great measure, by
preying on other animals; but this is a miserable way..."

(And miserable only leaves you wanting more.)

I, too, am a vegetarian in principle, if not always in
practice. I sometimes put pepperoni on my soy burgers!
And when I'm a guest at someone else's table, I eat
what's served. But that's usually it, because I don't like
taking advantage of advantage. And I know that I'm
stronger when everything weaker, well, is.

As for the woodchuck, Thoreau's review was mixed--

"It afforded me a momentary enjoyment, not
withstanding a musky flavor."

(Woody, we hardly knew ya!)

ORDINARY NOONS

"[P]ray what more can a reasonable man desire, in
peaceful times, in ordinary noons, than a sufficient
number of ears of green sweet corn...?"
--HENRY DAVID THOREAU, *WALDEN*

(Let's do lunch, T!)

SAVE YOUR FORK

Technically speaking, Thoreau didn't pay for all of the food he ate during his Walden days.

(Twenty-seven cents a week only went so far!)

Thoreau frequently dined at the Emerson's, for example.

And his mother and sister Sophia kept him well supplied with donuts and other home-made treats.

Cabin company, too, presumably, sometimes must've come bearing assorted flavorfuls.

"Wow, Purslane Waikiki!"

Some critics see this as disingenuous, a fudging of the *Walden* facts.

"He was a sponge."

I don't see it that way.

When I was starting out on my own (first apartment, first car, first student loan payment) and money was tight, my boss often treated me to lunch, my parents often bought me groceries, and my friends often took me for free appetizers at Friday's on Fridays.

Thanks, everybody!

(Burrrp.)

SOAKING IT UP

"To meet the objections of some inveterate cavillers, I may as well state, that if I dined out occasionally, as I always had done, and I trust shall have opportunities to do again, it was frequently to the detriment of my domestic arrangements."

--HENRY DAVID THOREAU, *WALDEN*

(Inveterate cavillers are the worst!)

HOME ALONE

Some people think that Thoreau was a recluse.

Bad rap!

While at Walden, he went into town every day or two, spending time with friends and acquaintances and checking in with family. He attended lectures and public meetings, kept in touch with the local literary circle, and was even known to take the village children out huckleberrying.

And Thoreau maintained an "open door" policy at his cabin, welcoming old pals and passersby alike. Emerson came often, as did William Ellery Channing, a companion whom I will introduce more formally 'ere long. Laborers chopping trees in the woods or cutting ice from the pond dropped in on Thoreau, too, occasionally using his place as a changing room!

Thoreau says in *Walden* that he sometimes had as many as twenty-five to thirty people under his cabin's roof!

(No comments about exaggerating crowd sizes, please.)

HIP, HIP, HOORAY

"I had three chairs in my house; one for solitude, two for friendship, three for society. When visitors came in larger and unexpected numbers there was but the third chair for them all, but they generally economized the room by standing up. It is surprising how many great men and women a small house will contain."
--HENRY DAVID THOREAU, *WALDEN*

R AND I

And some people think that Thoreau was selfish and self-absorbed.

While this is another misconception, Thoreau himself is to blame for it.

Thoreau writes at length in *Walden* about how he despised do-gooders and disapproved of organized philanthropic efforts--

"There are a thousand hacking at the branches of evil to

one who is striking at the root, and it may be that he who bestows the largest amount of time and money on the needy is doing the most by his mode of life to produce that misery which he strives in vain to relieve."

Reform and improve yourself, Thoreau would've said, before attempting to r and i others--

"Men say, practically, Begin where you are and such as you are, without aiming mainly to become of more worth, and with kindness aforethought go about doing good. If I were to preach at all in this strain, I should say rather, Set about being good."

That's the Transcendentalist talking.

Nevertheless...

Thoreau dabbled in do-good! He lent a helping hand to many a neighbor in need, proved to be a friend to the poor Irish immigrants building the railroads, and, as we shall see shortly, stepped up big time conducting runaway slaves to freedom.

Ah, yes, selfish and self-absorbed.

INTERVIEW WITH A GIRL SCOUT

"Thoreau"?

Yes, I knew Mr. Thoreau.

He always bought *all* of my cookies.

And all of my friends' cookies, too.

(Merit Badge City!)

He realized that if other people found out about it, they might start calling him a "do-gooder," and he would've totally hated that, but for Shortbreads, he was willing to take the risk.

HYDRATE!

Visitors to Thoreau's cabin would be offered a sip of their host's beverage of choice: water.

Thoreau wanted to keep his mind, and everybody else's, as clear as Walden Pond.

My doctor would've loved him! It seems the only thing about me that's above average is my blood pressure, so I'm supposed to limit my caffeine and alcohol.

It's been a challenge.

But I'm lucky to have my David to keep an eye on me, and he does, although I don't know how lucky he feels about having to do so.

("Because of my high bp, I'm H_2O sidelined.")

NOT SO NOBLE

"I believe that water is the only drink for a wise man;
wine is not so noble a liquor; and think of dashing the
hopes of a morning with a cup of warm coffee, or of an
evening with a dish of tea!"

--HENRY DAVID THOREAU, *WALDEN*

(Would it be okay, dash-wise, to add a slice of lemon?)

DID THOREAU S#IT IN THE WOODS?

As intriguing as Thoreau's domestic details may be,
they're only part of his story. Thoreau's cabin was a
means to an end. Our buddy had some issues, see, both
personal and professional, and he went to Walden to get
it together.

Beloved brother John, remember, had died three years
prior, and Thoreau was still trying to deal with that loss.
John had cut a finger while stropping a razor, developed
tetanus, and suffered an agonizing death. John breathed
his last in his brother's arms.

Thoreau wanted to write a book as a tribute to John
about a pleasure trip they'd taken via rough skiff to New
Hampshire's White Mountains in 1839. He'd tried, but
couldn't concentrate while living at home with the fam.
A Week on the Concord and Merrimack Rivers, which
Thoreau would publish in 1849, and which I'll come
back to later, was drafted during the Walden period.

(Oh, what I wouldn't give sometimes for an hour of Waldenesque peace&quietful writing--whoops, hold that thought: doorbell ringing, smoke alarm going off, and cat throwing up on the carpet...)

PURPOSE

"My purpose in going to Walden Pond was not to live cheaply nor to live dearly there but to transact some private business, with the fewest obstacles..."
--HENRY DAVID THOREAU, WALDEN

WALDEN, TOO

In addition to *A Week*, Thoreau managed to scribble out much of *Walden* at Walden, too.

He did so in response to popular demand--

"I should not obtrude my affairs so much on the notice of my readers if very particular inquiries had not been made by my townsmen concerning my mode of life, which some would call impertinent, though they do not appear to me at all impertinent, but, considering the circumstances, very natural and pertinent."

I can only imagine the buzz on social media...

"Walden Pond?!!! Pullleeease!"

"When's that boy gonna grow up and get a job?"

"Raisin bread?!!! LMAO!"

PEACE&QUIETFUL?

"At the approach of spring the red squirrels got under my house, two at a time, directly under my feet as I sat reading or writing, and kept up the queerest chuckling and chirruping and vocal pirouetting and gurgling sounds that ever were heard; and when I stamped they only chirruped the louder, as if past all fear and respect in their mad pranks, defying humanity to stop them."

--HENRY DAVID THOREAU, *WALDEN*

(I've heard a rumor that Thoreau caught the offending squirrels in one of those humane traps and released them in Emerson's backyard, but I haven't confirmed it yet.)

QUIET DESPERATION

Thoreau comments in *Walden* that "the mass of men lead lives of quiet desperation."

(Women are exempt?)

He'd heard his neighbors moaning, droning to pay their rents and mortgages, clothe and feed their families, and otherwise satisfy their "obligations"--

"How many a poor immortal soul have I met well-neigh crushed and smothered under its load creeping down the road of life..."

(Ugh!)

Walden was Thoreau's infomercial on It Don't Hafta Be.

While everybody else was crankin', he'd punched out early and gone off to cogitate--

"I am convinced, both by faith and experience, that to maintain one's self on this earth is not a hardship but a pastime, if we live simply and wisely."

Thoreau came to think that we've much to re-think.

That many of our To Do's should be left to'ed.

And, as we've seen, he practiced what he preached.

But did that, therefore, make him depression free?

There's an anxious tone in much of his writing that sounds suspiciously clinical to me--

"Men think that it is essential that the Nation have commerce, and export ice, and talk through a telegraph, and ride thirty miles an hour, without a doubt, whether they do or not; but whether we should live like baboons or like men, is a little uncertain."

(Take a deep breath, T!)

Thoreau was an idealist, and that's not always ideal. Common side effects include a sudden urge to scream, cry, or sigh. No, he never gave up hoping that humanity would stop racing around like rats, but he didn't seem to expect that to happen anytime soon.

INTERVIEW WITH A QUACK

"Thoreau"?

Why, he used to be one of my patients!

Struggled with QD.

("Quiet Desperation.")

I prescribed some medication, but it gave him constipation.

And there was a big co-pay.

So he decided to go the alternative route.

Haven't heard from him since.

Hope he's feeling better.

"Am I familiar with HIPPA"?

No, what's that?

57

MEETING TUESDAY @ 10 AM
W/ MS. BEECH & MR. BIRCH

Thoreau's interest in nature was intense and personal.

As he reveals in *Walden*--

*"I frequently tramped eight or ten miles through the
deepest snow to keep an appointment with a beech tree,
or a yellow birch, or an old acquaintance among the
pines."*

(Why not videoconference instead?)

Thoreau had acquired an encyclopedic knowledge of the
natural world. The plants and animals, the earth and sky,
the weather, the seasons. At times his writings read like
a scientific journal--

*"One afternoon I amused myself by watching a barred
owl sitting on one of the lower dead limbs of a white
pine, close to the trunk, in broad daylight, I standing
within a rod of him. He could hear me when I moved
and crunched the snow with my feet, but could not
plainly see me. When I made noise he would stretch
out his neck, and erect his neck feathers, and open his
eyes wide; but their lids soon fell again, and he began to
nod. I too felt a slumberous influence after watching him
half an hour..."*

(Half an hour?!!!)

But there's always a spiritual element as well.

COMPLEMENTAL VERSE

Woodchucks, rabbits, and squirrels
I spy
lurking 'round my cabin!
Come close, stay, don't giggle
while I
look, observe, examine.

Thoreau found more inspiration in a snowstorm than a sermon, and said so.

(What the saints and masters call "the finger of God"?)

THE WIND ON OUR CHEEKS

"Talk of mysteries! -- Think of our life in nature, -- daily to be shown matter, to come into contact with it,-- rocks, trees, wind on our cheeks! the SOLID earth! the ACTUAL world! the COMMON sense! CONTACT! CONTACT! WHO are we? WHERE are we?"

--HENRY DAVID THOREAU, *THE MAINE WOODS*

ECO-URGENCY

Thoreau was one of the first to suggest that we need to be more environmentally aware, responsible, and engaged.

The earth will continue to take care of us only if we continue to take care of it!

As Thoreau says in his essay "Life Without Principle"--

"If a man walk in the woods for love of them half of each day, he is in danger of being regarded as a loafer; but if he spends his whole day as a speculator, shearing off

those woods and making earth bald before her time, he is
esteemed an industrious and enterprising citizen. As if a
town had no interest in its forests but to cut them down!"

In Thoreau's writings, you can sense the eco-urgency.

And that was over a hundred and fifty years ago!

If only more people had listened.

If only more would.

LISTEN

"Who hears the fish when they cry?"
--HENRY DAVID THOREAU,
A WEEK ON THE CONCORD AND MERRIMACK RIVERS

ENVIRONMENTAL STEWARDSHIP

In 1989, two large real estate developments were
proposed for some of the land surrounding Walden Pond,
but singer-songwriter Don Henley and others raised
money to purchase the property, and additional adjoining
properties, before it was too late. The Walden Woods
Project, a non-profit conservation and educational
organization, was formed to preserve and protect the
area while spreading a message of "environmental
stewardship and social responsibility," as per its website,

www.walden.org.

(Check it out and /donate!)

A CENTURY HENCE

"I fear that he who walks over these fields a century hence will not know the pleasure of knocking off wild apples. Ah, poor man...!"
--HENRY DAVID THOREAU, "WILD APPLES"

(Knocking on, T!)

CAT PERSON

Personally, I categorize Thoreau as a cat person. Not that he didn't like dogs equally as well, I'm sure, without a doubt, so spare me your emails please, but he definitely had a cat-like curiosity, and that wildness-in-waiting way which even sheltered shelter cats display, an always-ready-to-pounce bounce.

As Thoreau himself notes in *Walden*--

"[T]he most domestic cat, which has lain on a rug all her days, appears quite at home in the woods, and, by her sly and stealthy behavior, proves herself more native there than the regular inhabitants."

Why, that's our guy!

David and I once had a cat who never went outside, by choice, except for visits to the vet, not by choice. We'd adopted her from the Rescue League when she was a year old. She was a timid little thing who'd been abused as a kitten. For the longest time, she hid under our couch and only came out to eat and use the litter box when we were both asleep in bed, but eventually she learned to trust us. We named her Cosette because she reminded us of the sad orphan in *Les Mis.*

Cosette was tiny enough to sit comfortably on a window ledge, and she did so every morning to watch the sun rise. She seemed to know exactly when to be at her post, and rarely let anything prevent her. Her face would light up, and not just literally, at first sight of the sun each day, but even when the sky was cloudy, she was faithful.

Always frail and sickly, Cosette suffered a heart attack early one morning in her sixth year. As David and I rushed to get dressed so that we could rush her to the animal hospital, she dragged herself to the new sun's beam that had just begun to seam the carpet, and quietly passed.

DOUBT NOT

"It is true, I never assisted the sun materially in his rising, but doubt not, it was of the last importance only to be present at it."

--HENRY DAVID THOREAU, *WALDEN*

SIMPLIFY

Thoreau was a master of time management.

Anyone who's ever attended a "Help! I Can't Cope!" seminar knows that the trick is prioritizing.

Plan to do your most important tasks first, your lesser important tasks thereafter, eliminating entirely any tasks that aren't really necessary.

Thoreau was all about "aren't really necessary."

As he advises in *Walden*--

"Simplicity, simplicity, simplicity! I say, let your affairs be as two or three, and not a hundred or a thousand; instead of a million count half a dozen, and keep your accounts on your thumb nail."

Whenever I can get my own "affairs" list down to a hundred or a thousand, I consider it a good day!

Which is why my blood pressure is high.

Pfft.

I hate it when Thoreau is right!

("I tried thumb-nail accountancy, but my manicurist undermined.")

MARGINAL NOTE

"I love a broad margin to my life."

--HENRY DAVID THOREAU, *WALDEN*

(Try reformatting!)

FULL DISCLOSURE

Okay, I'm a city hag!

(There, I've said it.)

Give me the big's, busy's, and booming's!

With their comforts, conveniences, and modern's.

It's who I am.

It's who I've always been.

I grew up on Clematis Street in Providence, RI, but there weren't many *clematides* on my urban block. It was one street down from Lawn, which didn't have much greened ground, and not far from Redwood, Robin, and River, which didn't, didn't, and didn't, either.

And in all my years, I haven't wandered very far for very long.

(Security probably wouldn't let me back in if I did!)

But I have to think that it's possible for *me*, too, here and now, *anywhere* and *always*, to front onlys, to discover life in *my* woods. On the go, on the grid, on the parade route. At work, at play, at the café. By trying to live, choose, acquire, use, value, spend, enjoy, attend, respect, protect, and question-and-answer more thoughtfully.

Waking up!

No, not exactly a *Walden* simplicity sim, but similar?

* * *

I WOULD FAIN SAY SOMETHING TO THOSE
OF YOU WHO LIVE IN THE CITY

Support community recycling programs.

Avoid dusty paperweights and other clutter
in home and office.

Streamline wardrobe to workable essentials,
donating decent discards to charity.

Opt for natural foods which require
less processing and prep.

Walk, car pool, or public tranp whenever possible.

And always break for squirrels, girl scouts, and sunrises.

Hit the pavement!

FRONTING ONLYS

"I awoke to an answered question."
--HENRY DAVID THOREAU, *WALDEN*

SITTING ON A PUMPKIN

Which brings me back to Thoreau's *Walden* take on
Keeping Up with the Whomever's--

*"Most men appear never to have considered what a
house is, and are actually though needlessly poor all
their lives because they think that they must have such a
one as their neighbors have."*

("I live in a bigger, more beautiful...")

How easily living becomes living better than!

As Thoreau quips--

"None is so poor that he need sit on a pumpkin."

But if None *were* and *did*...

Wouldn't he want the biggest, most beautiful pumpkin?
And a few more nice ones for guest seating? And a few
more still for end-tables?

And a chic rug from IKEA.

And...

SUMMING UP

In the end, *Walden* isn't about the cabin.

Or the pond.

Or even Thoreau.

It's about you and me.

DIVERSIFY

"I would not have any one adopt my mode of living on any account; for, beside that before he has fairly learned it I may have found out another for myself, I desire that there may be as many different persons in the world as possible; but I would have each one be very careful to find out and pursue his own way, and not his father's or his mother's or his neighbor's instead."
--HENRY DAVID THOREAU, *WALDEN*

INTERVIEW WITH A MUSICIAN

"Thoreau"?

Are you kidding me?

He was one of my biggest fans!

I'm the "different drummer" he wrote about.

(Or so I tell everybody!)

It's made my career, too.

Chartbuster CD's, sold-out concerts, my own line of band instruments...

(Just glad Ringo didn't think of it first.)

"What's next"?

The Thoreau School for Young Percussionists.

(Giving back, ya know?)

CABIN FEVER

Thoreau left Walden in late summer 1847.

He'd been there two years, two months, and two days.

Emerson was heading off to Europe on a lecture tour and he'd offered Thoreau a house-sitting position while he was gone.

Thoreau's Walden experiment had been open-ended, and his decision to bring it to a close appears to have been no big deal.

(Yawn.)

AS GOOD A REASON

"I left the woods for as good a reason as I went there. Perhaps it seemed to me that I had several more lives to live, and could not spare any more time for that one."
--HENRY DAVID THOREAU, *WALDEN*

EMPTY AND IDLE

Thoreau was the first and only occupant of his iconic cabin, as documented by Walter Harding.

Upon move-out, Thoreau sold the structure to Emerson, who in turn sold it to his gardener. Subsequent attempts to enlarge and reconfigure the place left it an unsafe ruin. It eventually was relocated to a nearby farm and used to store grain and other items until finally being dismantled and recycled as scrap.

Today, the Concord Museum has some cabin remnants-- a few small pieces of wood, bits of plaster and brick, and numerous nails.

THOREAU'S CABIN SITE

Walden Pond State Reservation
Concord, MA

Detroit Publishing Company Photograph
1908

Library of Congress
Gift of the State Historical Society of Colorado

A PLACE OF INTEREST

In time, Thoreau's cabin site became a place of interest to *Walden* fans, although the footprint had been obscured by grass and other overgrowth.

Visitors, including Walt Whitman in 1881, left small rocks as tokens of their devotion, eventually forming a large cairn.

(See photo on previous page.)

Excavations by Roland Wells Robins in 1945 uncovered the former cabin's exact location.

(It was a few feet away from the cairn, actually.)

When I visited last, the 10 x 15 plot was delineated by some stone posts connected by iron chains.

(I think Thoreau would've liked the grass and other overgrowth better.)

INTERVIEW WITH AN APPRAISER

"Thoreau"?

Yeah, I came across some of his cabin stuff once.

Two doorknobs, a shower head, and a ceiling fan.

Emerson's gardener brought them in.

I estimated that the lot would fetch $28.12½.

By the way, gardener guy said he also has Thoreau's Keurig, wine rack, and pool table.

(The Keno brothers would freak!)

IT WAS A CABIN

And before we, too, leave *Walden*, let me clarify one thing: Thoreau never called his cabin a "cabin," always a "house" or "dwelling."

But this is my book, and I'll do what I want.

JAMBLICHUS?

And speaking of *my* books, reviewers often gripe that I go off on tangents.

What can I say--I have an all-terrain brain.

And, let me add, sometimes random ain't so random.

(Incidentally, according to *Merriam-Webster*, "gripe" is one of the oldest words in the English language, having come into use sometime before the twelfth century...)

Well, everybody, Thoreau tended to tangents, too, especially in *A Week on the Concord and Merrimack Rivers*. As I've said, *A Week* is ostensibly about an "excursion" made in a rowboat. Thoreau and his brother John out on the water, the sun playing on its surface, fish, birds, *pontederia*, paddle paddle paddle, pant pant pant, pass a PowerBar, please!

And it makes for some mighty fine reading--

"We glided noiselessly down the stream, occasionally driving a pickerel or a bream from the covert of the pads, and the smaller bittern now and then sailed away on sluggish wings from some recess in the shore."

But there's also a ton of cut-and-paste philosophy, Eastern and Western, and poetry and literature, including a scene from *Antigone*, and local history, some of it drawn from funky old folktales, and musings on God and religion, and accounts of similar trips already completed, contemplated, or imagined...

There's even some Jamblichus!

(Because why not.)

And at some point along the way, *A Week* turns into the maiden voyage of Thoreau's flagship, *Walden*--

"What, after all, does the practicalness of life amount to? The things immediate to be done are very trivial. I could postpone them all to hear the locust sing....

*I would give all the wealth of the world, and all the
deeds of all the heroes, for one true vision.* "

Whenever David and I go on vacation, I usually need a
couple of days before I can put enough mental distance
between my "things immediate" and me to be able to
relax, enjoy, and just be.

"Yooou've got mail!"

Why is it like that?

Or, rather, why am I?

This is the wisdom of *A Week* for me.

(My one true vision and it's not even mine.)

HERE TOO

My favorite oddity in *A Week* is a tombstone engraving
that Thoreau quotes:

> *"Here lies an honest man,*
> *Rear-Admiral Van.*
> *Faith, then ye have*
> *Two in one grave,*
> *For in his favor,*
> *Here too lies the Engraver."*

(No idea.)

IN STOCK

A Week on the Concord and Merrimack Rivers was Thoreau's first book.

No publisher would chance it unless Thoreau paid the production costs up-front.

As you might expect, that was a snag.

(Should've tried GoFundMe.)

But Thoreau was able to work out a payment agreement, and *A Week* was.

Alas, it didn't become a bestseller.

(Although it did outsell my own first book, and my second, and probably will this my third.)

Before long, Thoreau's publisher deemed *A Week* a waste of warehouse space, and shipped its author the remaining inventory. Thoreau would joke thereafter that he had 900 books in his library, over 700 of which he'd written himself.

INTERVIEW WITH A PUBLISHING REP

"Thoreau"?

He once sent me a manuscript for consideration.

A Week on the Concord and Merrimack Rivers.

(Worst week of my life!)

But as I told him, we already have all the hot new authors we can handle.

(Most of whom we've been publishing for years.)

I wouldn't mind taking on that Jamblichus, though!

Know how I can get in touch with him?

UGLY AS SIN

Hawthorne once wrote that Thoreau was "ugly as sin."

(Ouch!)

I'm not sure I would go that far.

The pictorial evidence consists of some portraits drawn by friends and family and a few photos.

(See pages 11 and 119.)

Yes, Thoreau had a large nose, bad hair, and scary sideburns and beard.

But he had *dreamy* eyes!

The gaze of a poet.

Burning hotly, yet not hot, softer than felt, feeling.

Seeing seeing seeing.

(Did you just blink?)

Glimpsing the Over-Soul.

FASHION SENSE

Thoreau wasn't on any "best-dressed" lists, either.
Those who knew him, in fact, judged him to be more of
a hot mess!

Emerson, for example, once said that Thoreau's trousers
were "strong" and his shoes "stout." Not adjectives
commonly used by popular brands in marketing their
apparel.

And Thoreau himself tells us in *Walden* that he favored
clothing that was functional. Keep ya warm, keep ya
dry, keep ya privates private. Check, check, big check.

Thoreau's active, loose-fitting lifestyle required
garments to match. He never knew when he'd want to
plow through heavy brush, crawl in mud, or climb a tree.

(Well, duh!)

And he realized, too, that designer clothes, like most so-called "best's," usually aren't cheap.

Thoreau wasn't willing to toil away in an office so that he could afford to dress appropriately to toil away in an office.

Casual Fridays notwithstanding.

(I Google'd "strong trousers" for kicks, but we'd better not go there!)

GOOD ENOUGH

"No man ever stood the lower in my estimation for having a patch on his clothes; yet I am sure that there is greater anxiety, commonly, to have fashionable, or at least clean and unpatched clothes, than to have a sound conscience. But even if the rent is not mended, perhaps the worst vice betrayed is improvidence. I sometimes try my acquaintances by such tests as this,--Who could wear a patch, or two extra seams only, over the knee? Most behave as if they believed that their prospects for life would be ruined if they should do it. It would be easier for them to hobble to town with a broken leg than with a broken pantaloon. Often if an accident happens to a gentleman's legs, they can be mended; but if a similar accident happens to the legs of his pantaloons, there is no help for it; for he considers, not what is truly respectable, but what is respected."

--HENRY DAVID THOREAU, *WALDEN*

SECRET COMPARTMENT

Thoreau sometimes wore a large hat with a secret compartment inside for storing specimens that he picked up during his nature walks.

Animal, vegetable, mineral.

(Some of which are now in museums.)

Think what he could've accomplished with cargo pants!

INTERVIEW WITH A SEAMSTRESS

"Thoreau"?

Yes, I had *dealings* with him!

He came into my shop one day looking for some new clothes.

Easy as threading a needle, right?

So I took his measurements. Neck, waist, arms, legs. When I'd finished, he asked if I wanted to measure his "character" as well.

Don't talk dirty to a woman with shears, I warned him.

(Snip!)

I then suggested a few stylish things, but he pooh-pooh'ed them all.

Said he didn't want to look like a Parisian monkey.

(Frankly, I think that would've been an improvement.)

Before long, I'd had enough.

"Sorrrrry!"

I referred him to Filene's Basement.

As the Good Book says, "And on the sixth day, God created off-the-rack for slobs like him."

A STAMP

The U.S. Postal Service issued a stamp this year in recognition of Thoreau's 200th.

They wanted to honor him, but…

AND A STOMP

"For my part, I could easily do without the post-office. I think that there are very few important communications made through it."
--HENRY DAVID THOREAU, *WALDEN*

MAIL FRAUD

When I went to the P.O. to buy some of the new Thoreau
stamps, the sales associate asked "Who *was* he?"

"The inventor of raisin bread."

"Oh! Well, I could've guessed from his picture that it
wasn't disposable razors."

(Don't worry, I followed up with a better, if brief, bio--
Walden, simplify, reflect, relish, recycle; but stamp lady
remained most impressed by the raisin bread.)

Now I'll probably never get a stamp of my own, but let it
be known, I'm available.

I'll shave extra close!

Hell, I'll get a full body wax!

("Speaking philatelically, I aspire to be enshrined!")

OH!

*"Great men, unknown to their generation, have their
fame among the great who have preceded them, and all
truly worldly fame subsides from their high estimate
beyond the stars."*

--HENRY DAVID THOREAU,
A WEEK ON THE CONCORD AND MERRIMACK RIVERS

SEND E-CARD TO PRINCESS A.

Thoreau wasn't fond of the telegraph or newspapers, either.

(I think we can assume that he would've slammed phones, internet, and TV, too, except perhaps for *Nature, NOVA,* and *This Old House*.)

Thoreau wasn't convinced that enhanced methods of communication would enhance communication.

As he writes in *Walden*--

"Our inventions are wont to be pretty toys, which distract our attention from serious things. They are but improved means to an unimproved end.... We are in great haste to construct a magnetic telegraph from Maine to Texas; but Maine and Texas, it may be, have nothing important to communicate.... We are eager to tunnel under the Atlantic and bring the Old World some weeks nearer to the New; but perchance the first news that will leak through into the broad, flapping American ear will be that the Princess Adelaide has the whooping cough."

While I myself hold that an unplugged life is no longer worth living, I get it. Technology, like everything else, including our brains, ought to be used wisely and responsibly.

But that Princess Adelaide comment crossed the line!

OFF ON A TANGENT

Unlike Thoreau, Emerson wasn't born in Concord.

A commemorative plaque outside what is now Macy's department store in downtown Boston marks his birthplace.

(See photo on opposite page.)

David thinks that Emerson's mom must've been out shopping for baby clothes when she went into labor.

(She should've stayed home and ordered from the catalog!)

SURVEYING

Thoreau was a sometimes land surveyor. He was largely self-taught. His services were always in great demand, but, as we know, he wasn't exactly a workaholic, so he surveyed only occasionally.

Some of Thoreau's maps (or whatever they are called) are still around and are much admired by those in the profession.

But surveying presented a dilemma for Thoreau, as Walter Harding pointed out. Yes, he was discovering, exploring, and documenting new fields, woods, and

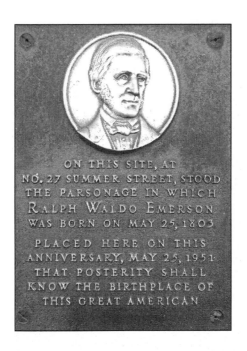

ON THIS SITE, AT
NO. 27 SUMMER STREET, STOOD
THE PARSONAGE IN WHICH
RALPH WALDO EMERSON
WAS BORN ON MAY 25, 1803

PLACED HERE ON THIS
ANNIVERSARY, MAY 25, 1951
THAT POSTERITY SHALL
KNOW THE BIRTHPLACE OF
THIS GREAT AMERICAN

PLAQUE MARKING EMERSON'S BIRTHPLACE

Outside Macy's
Summer Street
Boston, MA

out-of-the-way's, but he was also participating in their "development."

Funny story: Thoreau once surveyed some of Emerson's property and determined that it wasn't Emerson's property...

(Uh-oh!)

When I was growing up, my dad worked occasionally as a land surveyor, too. He was U.S. Army trained and true. Dad spent his week behind a desk, so he enjoyed "getting out in the field" on Saturdays. Since he often had to go where no plumber had gone before, he carried his own drinking water in a canteen. Dad always saved a few drops for my brother and me to slurp when he returned home. Yes, it was water from our kitchen tap that we could've had by the gallon, but somehow it tasted of the great outdoors.

SCREENING

In *Walden*, Thoreau submits a tongue-in-cheek résumé--

"For many years I was self-appointed inspector of snow-storms and rain-storms, and did my duty faithfully."

As an HR Manager, I've known worse!

People have "exaggerated" degrees, certifications, jobs, bosses, even entire companies.

"So, Mr. Thoreau, as part of our pre-employment screening, we'd like to get a reference from your former supervisor, Jack Frost..."

WHO'LL PLAY US IN THE MOVIE?

There have been a few films about Thoreau to date, mostly short indies, but no blockbusters yet. David and I sometimes dream that DreamWorks will get to work on a major motion picture based on this my book.

Who'll play Thoreau?

Kermit the frog.

Next!

More importantly, who'll play *us*?

I'm thinking Ed Harris and Tom Hanks, in either order.

David says Jonathan Groff him, Betty White me.

INTERVIEW WITH A HOLLYWOOD PRODUCER

"Thoreau"?

No, I don't know him, but I wish I did!

I'd love to do a *Walden* spinoff.

Here's my concept: the ax that Thoreau used when building his cabin shows up later at a horrible crime scene. There are bloody dismembered bodies everywhere. The cops examine the murder weapon and find multiple sets of fingerprints. Thoreau's, Emerson's, and Louisa May Alcott's, of course. But wait... Queen Victoria's! Anna Karenina's! Polly Wolly Doodle's! You see where I'm going with this?

A Nineteenth Century Fox whodunit!

Add a romantic sub-plot, a magic hula hoop, and some dinosaurs, and you've got money in the bank.

"I'd like to thank the Academy..."

LGBTQ?

Some people speculate that Thoreau might've been gay. John Schuyler Bishop's 2013 novel *Thoreau in Love*, for example, sizzles with same-sex sex. But as much as I'd like to include Thoreau on the LGBTQ team roster, I'm not certain that he was ever formally designated for assignment.

We know, for example, that Thoreau once proposed marriage to a woman. This is backed up by a letter and some comments Thoreau made in his journal. (This hetero apropo was a no-go.) And although Thoreau doesn't appear to have been a player, another woman once proposed marriage to him! (This time, Thoreau was the whoa.)

On the other hand, Thoreau did write an animated poem about an adolescent male student of his--

"Lately, alas, I knew a gentle boy,
Whose features all were cast in Virtue's mold,
As one she had designed for beauty's toy,
But after manned him for her own stronghold..."

But the experts usually interpret these venerative verses as platonic.

???

Thoreau himself states in *Walden* that he was happiest alone--

"To be in company, even with the best, is soon
wearisome and dissipating. I love to be alone. I never
found the companion that was so companionable as
solitude."

And when he uses the word "love" in his writings, it's most often directed toward the weather, the woods, or the wild. Or virtue, truth, or beauty in the abstract.

So asexual then?

Maybe.

But what are we to make of William Ellery Channing?

WEC was Thoreau's BFF. They were close in age and had similar interests. The two often hung around together, frequently took long walks together, and sometimes even slept-over together.

(Well, they did.)

Okay, none of that proves anything.

Yes, Channing had a wife and children, but he didn't co-habit with them much. In times of trouble, he turned to Thoreau for comfort and asked him on at least one occasion if he could move in with him, for "companionship."

(Well, he did.)

The poet Emma Lazarus (*"Give me your tired, your poor, your huddled masses yearning to breathe free..."*) met Channing when she visited Concord in 1876. It was fourteen years after Thoreau's death, but she found Channing still grieving. He spoke tenderly of his departed friend in terms a spouse might use as he led her on pilgrimage to the Walden cabin site.

LGBTQ or not, love is love, and Ellery Channing obviously felt it deeply.

I hope Thoreau did, too, in whatever way was his.

COMPLEMENTAL VERSE

I read it somewhere,
I dunno--
was it on a t-shirt?
I read it once, yeah,
and (hello!)
I really do believe it.

OPEN WIDE AND SAY AHHH!

In 2014, Harmony Ball Co. introduced a Thoreau
figurine as part of its fun Pot Belly collection of great
authors and others. It's 2.75 inches tall and made of
marble dust and resin. It appears to have been modeled
on the Maxham daguerreotype, and very well done, too.
You probably can still get one on Amazon for around
$15, if you're interested.

(But you'll have to dust it daily!)

The Pot Belly's all have removable heads, thereby
allowing one to examine their abdominal cavities.

(It may seem rude, but it's non-invasive.)

Deep down in Thoreau's gut is a mini-Walden Pond.

(Retaining water?)

WITHOUT RESERVATIONS

In 1849 and again in 1855, Thoreau and Ellery Channing
went to Cape Cod, "the bared and bended arm of
Massachusetts," trips which Thoreau would recount,
along with additional details from an 1850 solo, in a
book called, big surprise, *Cape Cod.* It's stuffed with
beach-grass, driftwood, and plovers, and peppered with
salty CC-ers, "often at once farmers and sea-rovers." It's

an amusing travelogue. Even readers who don't usually like Thoreau, usually love *Cape Cod*.

Thoreau and Channing didn't purchase a plane, hotel, and rental car package from Expedia. They took a steamer (boat) at the start and finish, but walked the rest of the long way. They found food and lodging wherever they could, sometimes in private homes with locals who didn't have reservations about welcoming weirdly whiskered wanderers without reservations--

"[Passing from Wellfleet to Truro, we] discovered two or three sober-looking houses... Their garrets were apparently so full of chambers, that their roofs could hardly lie down straight, and we had no doubt that there was room for us there."

When David and I were younger, we spent some time every summer in P-Town, short for Provincetown, located at the very tip of Cape Cod. It was an LGBTQ safe haven, one of the few places back then where we gays could hold hands, hug, and kiss in public--even dance together! That may not sound like much to teens through thirty-something's, but, believe me, it was everything.

As David and I walked around P-Town, I'd sometimes imagine Thoreau with us.

What would he have thought of the rainbow flags, pink boa'ed boys, and shops selling souvenirs, taffy, and sex toys! I fear our Commercial Street would've been too commercial for him, and our demonstrations of LGBTQity too demonstrative.

But I can assure you that David would've seized the opportunity to settle the "orientation question" once and for all.

"So listen, Hank, honey--what shall we do today? Go on a whale watching cruise or go to the Boatslip and cruise? You decide."

Very cagey.

ANKLE-DEEP

"In some pictures of Provincetown the persons of the inhabitants are not drawn below the ankles, so much being supposed to be buried in the sand."

--HENRY DAVID THOREAU, CAPE COD

(Never wear stilettos in the dunes, ladies!)

WANTED!

During Thoreau's 1850 trip to Cape Cod, the bank in P-Town was robbed. Thoreau became a Most Wanted for a while, until the police caught the real crook.

But this wasn't Thoreau's first run-in with the law...

Na-ahh.

BUSTED!

Thoreau had been jailed once, as I've mentioned, for willful failure to pay his taxes. This had occurred on July 24th or 25th, 1846, one year into his Walden residency.

The suspect was apprehended while traveling on foot in the vicinity of Concord village and was taken into custody by Sam Staples, constable. He was unarmed and yielded without a struggle to the arresting officer.

Thoreau gives an account of this incident in an essay that's come to be known as "Civil Disobedience." Today, *Walden* + "CD" = Thoreau's claim to fame.

Thoreau owed *six years* of poll taxes, an important source of government funds in those days, but it wasn't because he couldn't pay. And even if that had been the prob, he knew that others were willing to pay for him-- Sam Staples himself had offered to do so! No, Thoreau was pissed at the Powers that Be'd, and his act/non-act was a protest.

Thoreau tells us in "CD" that he had two primary policy objections: (1) slavery and (2) the war then being fought by the U.S. with Mexico which he and many others feared would result in an extension of slavery.

Thoreau opens his essay with a bold declaration--

"I heartily accept the motto: 'That government is best which governs least...'"

Said "motto," of uncertain origin, usually continues:

"...because its people discipline themselves."

Ah!

Thoreau left that last part out, but I'm inking it back in.

Thoreau goes on to state that the best state would be to have no State, and criticizes anybody who wants a State for reasons of "public tranquility" and "protection."

That'd be me!

As a gay man, I know from personal, painful experience that other people don't always "discipline themselves." I can't be certain, in fact, that without a government to protect me, others won't deny my rights and freedoms, try to forcibly "convert" me, or even confine or kill me. Sadly, discrimination, disenfranchisement, and hateful acts of violence are a discipline to some.

Not everybody, of course, and not even most, thank God, but it probably wouldn't take many, and, I fear, there'd be more than enough.

And Thoreau seemed to understand this, too--

"But, to speak practically and as a citizen, unlike those who call themselves no-government men, I ask for, not at once no government, but at once a better government."

Now you're talking!

That's something we can all work toward together, and *should*, starting yesterday.

Thoreau's tax protest was his way of withholding support, both financially and morally, from a government he couldn't buy into, if you'll pardon the expression, to "refuse allegiance" and "stand aloof," and he was willing to be jailed for his resistance. If enough people followed his example, he reasoned, they would "clog" the "machinery" of government, and change would be inevitable--

"If the alternative is to keep all just men in prison, or give up war and slavery, the State will not hesitate which to choose."

Thoreau called his approach a "peaceable revolution." It would be adopted by others after him, including Mahatma Gandhi and his followers in India in the 1940's and the Rev. Dr. Martin Luther King, Jr. and his fellow civil rights activists here in the States during the 1960's.

Peace *can* work!

STILL.

Long story short...

Somebody paid Thoreau's taxes anonymously.

(Most finger his Aunt Maria.)

And Thoreau was released from jail after less than a day,

more than a little annoyed--

"If others pay the tax which is demanded of me, ... from a mistaken interest in the individual taxed, ... it is because they have not considered wisely how far they let their private feelings interfere with the public good."

(My lips are sealed, Maria!)

Legend has it that when Emerson asked Thoreau later why he'd gone to jail, Thoreau asked Emerson why he hadn't.

(Zero points, Waldo.)

SO THERE I WAS, MINDING MY OWN BUSINESS, WHEN ALL OF A SUDDEN...

"I was put into jail as I was going to the shoemaker's to get a shoe which was mended. When I was let out the next morning, I proceeded to finish my errand, and, having put on my mended shoe, joined a huckleberry party, who were impatient to put themselves under my conduct; and in half an hour--for the horse was soon tackled--was in the midst of a huckleberry field, on one of our highest hills, two miles off, and then the State was nowhere to be seen."
--HENRY DAVID THOREAU, "CIVIL DISOBEDIENCE"

(If only Thoreau had called those 1-800 people who will help settle a tax debt for a fraction of what is owed, all this unpleasantness could've been avoided.)

98

INTERVIEW WITH A GANGSTER

"Thoreau"?

Yeah, I met him in the slammer.

"Nosey Nellie" I used to call him.

Seemed a little *too* interested in what I'd done to get locked up.

(Hadda be a plant!)

I told him to back off or he'd find himself swimming with the fishes.

He said that was one of his favorite things!

We'll just see…

(Hey, I didn't talk to Capote, I certainly wasn't gonna spill my guts to him!)

SPEAKING OUT

In 1854, Thoreau gave a fiery lecture, which he soon published, entitled "Slavery in Massachusetts."

The Fugitive Slave Law required all states then, even the "free" ones like Massachusetts, to cooperate in restoring to their owners any fugitive slaves found within their borders. Thoreau saw this as unjust and spoke out to persuade others to his point.

In "Slavery," Thoreau takes aim at the law itself, but also at the Massachusetts governor, courts, and militia that were enforcing it. He also finds fault with the churches, the press, and the public who, in his view, were giving slavery their silent, passive consent.

And Thoreau warns of the consequences--

"A government which deliberately enacts injustice, and persists in it, will at length even become the laughing-stock of the world."

(Haven't I heard that on MSNBC recently?)

Thoreau was enraged by the case of Anthony Burns, a fugitive slave from Virginia who had been captured in Boston and was being held awaiting trial. The proceedings would cause unrest in the streets, including an unsuccessful rescue attempt in which a U.S. Marshall would be fatally stabbed.

It wasn't "an era of repose," to borrow a phrase from Thoreau.

(Anthony Burns was soon transported back to Virginia and re-enslaved. Some good Bostonians, however, were able to buy his freedom. He eventually became a Baptist preacher, until, sadly, he died from TB at twenty-eight.)

SILENT AND PASSIVE

"What I have to do is to see, at any rate, that I do not lend myself to the wrong which I condemn."

--HENRY DAVID THOREAU, "CIVIL DISOBEDIENCE"

ACTING UP

Thoreau, you may remember, was involved with the Underground Railroad, helping a number of runaway slaves to freedom in Canada. He arranged safe accommodations for them, attended to their personal needs, bought them train tickets, and saw them off, sometimes accompanying them part of the way.

It was all against the law, deliberately defiant, but, then, as Thoreau suggests in "Civil Disobedience"--

"Unjust laws exist: shall we be content to obey them, or shall we endeavor to amend them and obey them until we have succeeded, or shall we transgress them at once? Men, generally, under such a government as this, think that they ought to wait until they have persuaded the majority to alter them. They think that, if they should resist, the remedy would be worse than the evil. But it is the fault of the government itself that the remedy is worse than the evil. It makes it worse. Why is it not more apt to anticipate and provide for reform?"

I'm usually more "endeavor to amend" than "transgress

at once," but I'll admit Thoreau was the better man here.

Thoreau never got caught Underground Railroading, but he would've accepted the penalty and punishment if he had. He'd been to jail once already for the cause, albeit indirectly, and was willing to go again--

"Under a government which imprisons any unjustly, the true place for a just man is also a prison."

Could I have been as daring and heroic? I don't know. I can only hope so. I know I would've wanted to help, but that's not the same thing, is it?

O CHRISTIAN, WILL YOU SEND ME BACK?

"I had some guests [at the cabin on Walden Pond]..., one real runaway slave, among the rest, whom I helped to forward to the north star."
--HENRY DAVID THOREAU, *WALDEN*

GOING TOO FAR?

In 1859-60, Thoreau penned a set of lectures/essays in praise and support of John Brown, the abolitionist who led a raid on the federal arsenal at Harpers Ferry, Virginia (now West Virginia). Brown wanted to liberate the facility's slaves and take possession of the arms and ammunition that were being stored there, as part of a paramilitary campaign to end slavery. Brown was soon overpowered by a deployment of U.S. Marines under the command of the future-Confederate-general Robert E. Lee.

At least seven people died as a result of the raid.

Brown was tried for treason, insurrection, and murder, found guilty, and hanged.

Thoreau states bluntly his defense of Brown--

"It was [John Brown's] peculiar doctrine that a man has a perfect right to interfere by force with the slaveholder, in order to rescue the slave. I agree with him."

That "by force" scares me.

Rule by force means rule by the most forceful, not necessarily the most worthy.

Slavery was evil, our nation's greatest sin, and had to be stopped. But homosexuality is considered evil by a minority now, and some have threatened to en-" force" this prejudice, regardless of the law. Not good.

Today, as I'm writing this, August 12th, 2017, a man has driven a car into a crowd in Charlottesville, VA, killing one person and injuring thirty-five others. He was motivated, in part, by the planned relocation of a statue of Robert E. Lee which now stands in said town located about 150 miles from Harpers Ferry. His was a peculiar doctrine that he had a perfect right to interfere by force with those who held other beliefs, views, and opinions.

No, Thoreau didn't advocate violent attacks on unarmed civilians, but don't his John Brown writings pave a dangerous road?

Thoreau undoubtedly was on the right side of the slavery divide, but...

Condone "by force" and you'll have blood on your hands.

(Walter Harding noted that although Thoreau had met John Brown when he'd passed through Concord in 1858, he wasn't aware of Brown's previous participation in a massacre of Native Americans in Kansas. Harding speculated that a better informed Thoreau wouldn't have been so enamored of Brown and his methods.)

WHAT WE DO NOT KNOW

"It was through [John Brown's] agency, far more than anyother's, that Kansas was made free."
--HENRY DAVID THOREAU, "A PLEA FOR CAPTAIN JOHN BROWN"

(Free for *all*?)

STONEWALL

It's generally accepted that the LGBTQ "movement" started at Stonewall, a gay bar in New York City, on June 28th, 1969. On that night, patrons of the bar, mostly men, but including some women, fed up with harassment by the police, engaged in a spontaneous confrontation with law enforcement. They "fought back," with fists and feet and bottles and rocks.

Many people were injured, some seriously.

Stonewall became a rallying cry for LGBTQs. Activist groups formed everywhere, became visible, worked hard, sacrificed, challenged, risked, informed, reformed, and, gradually, and mostly peacefully, with the help and support of many non-LGBTQs, made better happen.

LGBTQ Pride celebrations across the globe now commemorate the anniversary of Stonewall, and the site is a National Historic Landmark.

I was only twelve years old on June 28th, 1969, nowhere near NYC, and largely unaware of matters LGBTQ. Nevertheless, most of the rights and privileges that I have as a gay man in 2017 are a direct result of that night of protest and what it all led to.

Still…

I struggle to be proud of Stonewall without disclaimers. Was it not a *riot*? Was it not violence? Was it not hate reflected?

Understandable.
Provoked.
"Time."

Yes.

But did that make it *right*?

Hmmm.

GONE PLOTTING

Thoreau is sub-categorized on Wikipedia under "Anarchy." It seems that just because a guy writes, as Thoreau does in "Slavery in Massachusetts," that he'd like to strike a match and "blow up" the "system," he's an anarchist.

(Sticks and stones!)

Emma Goldman, the original Ctrl-Alt-Delete, adored Thoreau. When she wasn't busy inciting civil incivility and inspiring political assassinations, she snuggled up with Thoreau's collected works.

I'll bet her favorite line was from "Slavery"--

"My thoughts are murder to the State, and involuntarily I go plotting against her."

BUT, Emma, sweetie…

Notice that "involuntarily."

(And put down your Molotov cocktail!)

Thoreau may've sent some bad Tweets about the

government, but, as we've seen, he didn't want to bring it down "at once"--and everything else with it.

He was never loath to confront, but he confronted Transcendentally.

Vandalism, looting, indiscriminate anything?

Not likely.

As I see it, Thoreau's only fault in this regard was his impatience with the process.

He dismissed the "ways" of government as too slow--

"I know not of such ways. They take too much time, and a man's life will be gone. I have other affairs to attend to."

Well, excuuuse me!

Back in the 1980's and 90's, David and I were active in the fight for LGBTQ rights here in Rhode Island. No, we didn't spear-head any efforts, but we marched, shouted, chanted, flier-ed, sign-ed, letter-ed, contacted, asked, petitioned, shared, explained, modeled, tried, cried, and came *way* out.

As did others, variously other-ed.

And we many one…

Blew up the system.

(Please close cover before striking!)

SAY AGAIN?

"I came into this world, not chiefly to make this a good place to live in, but to live in it, be it good or bad."
--HENRY DAVID THOREAU, "CIVIL DISOBEDIENCE"

(Sorry, T, but the way you lived your life proved just the opposite, and a damn good thing for the world, too!)

NOT YOUR SUPERHERO

Thoreau and Emerson became less of a dynamic duo as the years went by. Differences of temperament and opinion strained their once close relationship.

They both seemed to expect greater things from each other, and felt personally let down when their hopes weren't met.

This tension is central to *The Night Thoreau Spent in Jail,* a poignant 1970's drama by Jerome Lawrence and Robert E. Lee (not the Confederate general this time). In the play, Emerson promises Thoreau that he will deliver an anti-slavery address in Concord. Thoreau excitedly rings the church bell to gather the townspeople together. Emerson chickens out. Thoreau is crushed.

COMPLEMENTAL VERSE

To say "ALL PEOPLE ARE GOOD"
is to trust,
ain't no two ways about it.
But only then can we do what we should,
what we must,
so trust, please/thank you, and shout it!

But why?

After all, Thoreau had not-heard it all before.

And the stakes were high for Emerson.

He was loved, rich, and famous.

GIVE ME TRUTH

"Rather than love, than money, than fame, give me truth."
--HENRY DAVID THOREAU, *WALDEN*

A FAMILIAR STORY

In many respects, Thoreau witnessed the beginnings of our age.

Rampant commercialism, encroaching technologies, social and political instability, economic inequality, ecological insensitivity, moral and spiritual uncertainty...

It was now, only then.

As Thoreau puts it in *A Week*--

"This modern world is only a reprint."

What a mess we've made of it!

And Thoreau raged against everybody and everything he considered responsible. The government. The churches. "Soulless incorporated bodies."

Which is what I like most about him.

Because I rage, too.

You?

BIG IF

"What is the use of a house if you haven't got a tolerable planet to put it on?"
--HENRY DAVID THOREAU,
LETTER TO H. G. O. BLAKE, MAY 20TH, 1860

THE BATTLE OF THE ANTS

Thoreau spent a day at Walden Pond watching ants, some red, some black, having a fight, "a war between two races." He gives an account of the combat in *Walden*, with clever military references, but it's a shade graphic and gross, so don't say I didn't warn you--

"I watched a couple [of ants] that were fast locked in each other's embraces, ... now at noonday prepared to

fight till the sun went down, or life went out. The smaller red champion had fastened himself like a vice to his adversary's front, and through all the tumblings on that field never for an instant ceased to gnaw at one of his feelers near the root, having already caused the other to go by the board; while the stronger black one dashed him from side to side, and, as I saw on looking nearer, had already divested him of several of his members."

Thoreau tells us that he never learned what had caused the war or which side was ultimately victorious.

(How many of us could say the same about most recent human wars!)

Readers of my previous books know that I'm a pacifist. I don't believe that a just war is possible anymore. Not when non-combatants can't be kept safe. *"No other way"? "Kill or be killed"? "Strike first or you might not be around to strike at all"?*

That's ant thinking.

We can do better.

CHANGED INTO MEN

"Still we live meanly, like ants; though the fable tells us that we were long ago changed into men."
--HENRY DAVID THOREAU, *WALDEN*

INTERVIEW WITH AN ANT

"Thoreau"?

Wasn't he the guy who wrote that *Ant Wars* story?

Only he got it all wrong.

The "battle" he witnessed was staged!

We were making a miniseries for Netflix.

Rubber limbs, plastic heads, wire antennae.

Oh, and lots of ketchup.

"Conquer or die!"

(Great screenplay.)

Wait, you don't think we ants really fight among
ourselves like erect bipedal primates, do you?

I mean, where would *that* end?

READING

Thoreau was appalled by his neighbors' taste in books.

Read a classic, he quipped, and you won't find anybody
to discuss it with.

(So start a chat room.)

As Thoreau whines in *Walden*--

*"The best books are not read even by those who are
called good readers."*

(Must've been referring to *my* books!)

Thoreau belittled *Little Reading*, a then popular digest,
and mocked the growing passion for serial romances.

*"How will Squire Aidan choose between the Anderson
twins? To be continued... Next month's installment:
'Ménage à trois.'"*

(Okay, not a real quote.)

On a recent visit to Thoreau's hometown, I dropped by
the Concord Bookshop to investigate what the natives
were reading these days. John Grisham, Anita Shreve,
and J. K. Rowling all were in good supply. But there
were also a number of classics in stock, including a
"Local Authors" section featuring Henry David, Ralph
Waldo, and Louisa May.

And while there I got to meet Laura Dassow Walls,
whose new biography of Thoreau has been hailed as the
best written in fifty years.

"We know more now than we did then..." she told me.

Speak for yourself!

THE HOUSE IN WHICH THOREAU LIVED
FROM 1850 UNTIL HIS DEATH IN 1862

The Thoreau-Alcott House
255 Main Street
Concord, MA

Detroit Publishing Company Photograph
Circa 1900

Library of Congress
Gift of the State Historical Society of Colorado

(Anybody interested in Thoreau really should be reading Professor W's book instead of mine, but you didn't hear that from me!)

INTERVIEW WITH A PAPERBACK HACK

"Thoreau"?

Well, I don't like to brag, but I did write an awesome book about him!

Fronting Onlys.

(No, not a typo.)

I'm surprised you haven't heard of it!

My biography is totally fact-based.

Except for all the stuff that I made up.

No option!

Thoreau was duller than a dead woodchuck, so I had to give him an amusing back-story.

Red Sox fan.

Karaoke nut.

Who wants to be a Millionaire? finalist.

"*Moby Dick was___? a. a whale; b. a snail; c. an ale; d. a guy named Richard with big hands.*"

"*Gee, Regis, I think I'd like to phone a friend--Herman Melville.*"

Oh, yes.

Mission accomplished.

HOLY STOLI!

Leo Tolstoy gives Thoreau a nod in his 1899 novel *Resurrection.*

At 600 pages, it's practically a Tolstoy short story! No, it's not his best work, but it's better than anything of mine, in real time, so, whoop-de-do, fine.

Resurrection is about a Russian prince named Dmitri Ivanovich Nekhlyudov, a playboy who tracks from naughty to nice, with mixed results. After a disagreeable day of jury duty, he has a Transcendental moment. "Holy Stoli! It's like *déjà* Thoreau! *'Under a government which imprisons any unjustly, the true place for a just man is also a prison.'* So what am I doing still out on the streets? Somebody lock me up, and pronto, please!"

(As freely translated by *moi*.)

117

All joking aside…

Resurrection is really a great book, Nekhlyudov a great protagonist, and Thoreau a great name to drop.

(I should know!)

PERSPECTIVE

Thoreau helps me to keep my perspective.

As he once advised a friend in a letter--

"It is not enough to be industrious; what are you industrious about?"

No, I don't expect that I'll ever live in the middle of nowhere, support myself by the labor of my hands, and be able to pack all of my possessions into a single paragraph. Nor would I be happy alone for very long, with patches on my pants, dining on purslane.

(Let's not even talk Jamblichus!)

But I think there's something to be gained from learning to live more deliberately, challenging routines, attitudes, and assumptions, and keeping sight of the Big Picture. Not wanting so much of whatever, not wasting so much of whatever, and not worrying so much, like, *whatever*!

So when the masses rise against me…

HENRY DAVID THOREAU

(Age 44)

From an 1861 ambrotype by
Edward Sidney Dunshee.
Photograph created circa 1879.

Library of Congress

FACTITIOUS CARES

"Most men, ... through mere ignorance and mistake, are so occupied with the factitious cares and superfluously coarse labors of life that its finer fruits cannot be plucked by them."

--HENRY DAVID THOREAU, *WALDEN*

For more information, contact:
Tom Beattie
V.P. of Factitious Cares
Superfluously Coarse Labors Department

WOULD THOREAU HAVE LIKED ME?

Probably not!

I'm too much of a democrat for his taste.

(And a Democrat!)

But I think he would've liked my two cats.

(Everybody does.)

THE FOLLOWING PAGES

This past summer, the Morgan Library and Museum in New York mounted a special exhibition on Thoreau to celebrate his 200th. David and I managed to drop in one afternoon for a quick look-see.

Among the items on view were some of Thoreau's journals, jottings, and books, including a manuscript draft of the first page of *Walden*--

"When I wrote the following pages, or rather the bulk of them, I lived alone, in the woods, a mile from any neighbor, in a house which I had built myself, on the shore of Walden Pond, in Concord, Massachusetts..."

Wow!

If only Thoreau had known that his "following pages" would be followed by these *my* pages!

(Was I wrong not to offer the Morgan my cabin model for their exhibition?)

FINAL DAYS

Thoreau died on May 6th, 1862, a Tuesday, at 9 p.m.

He'd been struggling with TB for many months, years actually, with increasingly painful cough and breathing, physically slowing, thank you but no-ing, more introspective growing.

He was only forty-four.

Some lines from *Walden* have always struck me as prophetic--

"Time is but the stream I go a-fishing in. I drink at it; but while I drink I see the sandy bottom and detect how shallow it is."

Thoreau's family and friends filled his final days with love and care. His mother, sister Sophia, and Aunt Louisa nursed him ably to the end. Emerson, Hawthorne, and other chums visited, as did the ever devoted Ellery Channing.

Good classicist that he was, Thoreau accepted his fate stoically. Being sick wasn't much different than being healthy, he said. As he'd written in *Walden*--

"[P]etty fears and petty pleasures are but the shadow of the reality."

At some point, Auntie Lou urged her nephew to make his peace with God. Thoreau replied that he wasn't aware they'd ever quarreled.

Good one!

LEGACY

"Thus the pond recovered the greater part."
--HENRY DAVID THOREAU, *WALDEN*

UNDERSTOOD

I read in the newspaper recently that the counselor who put me through Thoreau de-programming back in the day has passed away.

May he rest in peace, my thoughts and prayers, with sincerest so forth's.

I made a small donation in his memory to the Friends of Walden Pond.

(Couldn't resist.)

INTERVIEW WITH A STATIONER

"Thoreau"?

Sure, I knew him.

He was one of my best customers.

Bought writing paper.

Tons of it.

Always "100% recycled post-consumer waste"!

He was an author, you know.

If you've never read *Walden*, you should.

HENRY

Thoreau is buried on Authors Ridge in Concord's Sleepy Hallows Cemetery, next to his parents, brother, and sisters.

His grave is marked by a small stone which reads, simply, "Henry."

(See photo on opposite page.)

I'm going to be cremated when I die, so I probably won't have a grave marker, but if I were to, I'd want a huuuge rock with a lengthy inscription--something like, say, "Devoted Spouse, Friend to Humankind, Champion of Lost Causes, Etc." And, of course, "Author of the International Best Seller *Fronting Onlys*."

David has promised to sprinkle some of my ashes on Authors Ridge in Concord's Sleepy Hallows Cemetery.

UNFRIENDED

Emerson dissed Thoreau in his funeral eulogy, suggesting that he'd wasted his considerable talents--

"Wanting [ambition], instead of engineering for all America, he was the captain of a huckleberry party."

Very nice.

THOREAU'S GRAVE

Authors Ridge
Sleepy Hallow Cemetery
Concord, MA

OOPS!

Whenever I'm having one of *those* days, which seems to be most days these days, I find encouragement in something Thoreau once taught, as recounted by Walter Harding, of course.

Thoreau had taken Emerson's young son Edward out to pick huckleberries. One the way home, the child tripped and fell, spilling his basket of berries in the grass.

Oops!

Edward was distraught and cried, until Thoreau explained that sometimes Mother Nature makes use of little boys thusly to ensure that there will be more huckleberries to pick in years to come.

It's a lesson of hope, of tomorrows, of beyond's.

I wonder if little Eddie ever mentioned the incident to his dad...

Probably not!

In Concord today, there are huckleberries *everywhere*.

Just saying.

A VISIT WITH A VISIONARY

"Thoreau"?

Yes, I am he.

But do call me "Henry," please.

Welcome to my dwelling!

Make yourself comfortable.

You're just in time to share my supper--

Bread and water.

"No"?

Suit yourself then.

"2017"?

Oh, incessant influx of novelty!

I've never entertained a visitor from the future before.

Tell me about your world...

Are people free to pursue their dreams? Do you live at peace with each other and one with Nature? Is there wonder, hope, and joy?

"No"?

Suit yourselves then.

SUCCESS

When I graduated from high school in 1975, my parents gave me a copy of *The Portable Thoreau* along with a bookmark that had a *Walden* quote on it--

"If the day and the night are such that you greet them with joy, and life emits a fragrance like flowers and sweet-scented herbs, is more elastic, more starry, more immortal--that is your success."

Best gift ever.

HACKING HENRY

The same sun that rose at Walden Pond this morning shown on the dashboard of my Jeep Liberty as I drove to work on I-95...

Your turn!

Peace,

Tom

October 4th, 2017
Providence, Rhode Island

WOODCHUCK #1

"Too late now to skip to the end!"

Depositphoto.com

"I have learned this, at least, by my experiment [at Walden Pond]: that if one advances confidently in the direction of his dreams, and endeavors to live the life which he has imagined, he will meet with a success unexpected in common hours. He will put some things behind, will pass an invisible boundary; new, universal, and more liberal laws will begin to establish themselves around and within him or the old laws be expanded, and interpreted in his favour in a more liberal sense, and he will live with the license of a higher order of beings. In proportion as he simplifies his life, the laws of the universe will appear less complex, and solitude will not be solitude, nor poverty poverty, nor weakness weakness. If you have built castles in the air, your work need not be lost; that is where they should be. Now put the foundations under them."

--HENRY DAVID THOREAU, *WALDEN*

WAKING

August 27th, 2017

"Arise and walk through the land in the length, and in the breadth thereof: for I will give it to thee."
--GENESIS 13:17

Today, a Sunday, early in the a.m., I went for a walk along the Blackstone River in Lincoln, Rhode Island, hoping it was not already too late to discover something SOMETHING, not in cathedral, church, or chapel, no offense, because the Bible tells me so, amen, alleluia, ironically, perhaps, despite good intentions, enough said, and done, to these, at least, the least, hoping, to repeat, to drag my feet, etcetera, to points a-pointing.

"And the spirit of God moved over the waters."
--GENESIS 1:2

To exercise body and soul.

The river, named for the Rev. William Blackstone (1595–1675), one of the area's earliest settlers, extends forty-eight miles from Worcester, MA, to just east of Providence, RI. It played a key role in the Industrial Revolution, powering manufactories and facilitating the transport of goods, textiles, mainly, forming communities and informing characters, who and what, by golly, becoming us, thus, and with what consequences, then and now, how it was and is, progress, and proud of it, good measure, our pleasure, no problem, enjoy!

In the early 1990's, the Environmental Protection Agency ranked the Blackstone as one of the most polluted waterways in the nation, but recent clean-up and preservation efforts have restored it to generally stable health. The patient has been detoxed and is showing signs of recovery, requiring on-going care, yeah, and the support of family and friends, commitment, a little luck, one day at a time, no dumping please, let's all do our part, like there's no tomorrow, because, if not, there won't be.

Today…

I begin my walk at the Blackstone River Visitor Center in Quinnville, one of the seven villages that make up the Town of Lincoln. The VC has free maps, educational exhibits, and a helpful staff willing and able to direct and advise, but I don't take aught of that or them, waiving to the Park greeters without stopping, restless and reckless, regrets only.

I set out immediately, heading south, sticking to the paved path known officially as the Bikeway, which winds, more or less, along the river, where, in spite of its name, cyclists are joined by pedestrians, joggers, and rollerbladers, each doing his/her own thing, not always, incidentally, without incident, the rule, walkers left, which doesn't seem right to many, more honored in the breach.

As people pass going in the opposite direction, I nod, smile, and say "hello," about half replying in some way, those who don't "in the zone," possibly, or otherwise lost in thought, probably, or unfriendly, plain and simple, or afraid, maybe, to engage with strangers, which may be wise, in some cases, and definitely sad.

The Bikeway is relatively flat and smooth, the Lincoln stretch, anyway, except where the asphalt has been cracked by tree roots beneath, but patched, and so repaired, by students of Jackson Pollock, apparently, with squiggly lines of black tar and yellow safety paint, nice touch, great job, and thanks.

Although it's still summer, I step on newly fallen leaves, crunching, and strips of tree bark, and pine cones, and, occasionally, candy bar wrappers and cigarette butts, used Band Aids and wads of chewed gum, too, sticking and sticky--

Focus!

There are mile markers along the way, for serious athletes, presumably, calculating, pace and splits, whatever, means something to them, cast in stone, standing blocky, exact and exacting, all about distance, covered. I start at Mile 11, ready, set, and go backwards, merrily arbitrarily, 10, 9, 8, great, fate, you do the math, just a number, really, solve for x, and why.

I approach Canoe Rock, so labeled, so I know, a natural formation looking like an upside-down boat to some, a place of special importance, my guess, to the Native

135

Americans who once inhabited these parts, Nipmuc or Wampanoag, or both, or neither, for meetings, rituals, or rest, perhaps, wish I knew, but that'll have to do, something to research anon.

I step over two giant footprints on the pavement, thirty-six inches toe to heal. Sasquatch? If so, he/she has two left feet and recently stepped in chalk--a hoax!

Before long, my senses kick into higher gear.

Listen!

The reverberation of the river, regular and comforting, a heartbeat, a secret whispered in the wind, on top of which, the sounds of the birds and other living things, living, a song sung, for anyone who has ears to hear, and cares.

Smell!

Is that air freshener? No, it's the scent of real flowers, and grapes, and apples, and... There's earth odors, too, a little *eeew*, like a potted plant watered, and even an occasional whiff of dung and dropped-dead decay, which, oddly, are an essential part of the whole.

Look!

The sun spots colors, shapes, and textures. High def! What a lot of greens, plural, nursery pinks and blues, and orangeredbrowns. Dappled, wrote the poet, vintage

Disney, as I know it, variegated, no two alike, how cool is that! Trees and shrubs, already primping for their Fall Ball, grasses and ferns, mushrooms, bearing but slight resemblance to those that come in a can or jar, and wildflowers, lacey, ribboned, and assorted jelly-beaned, buttoned, snapped, and zippered, a handful of crayons, or Q-Tips, white and cottony, crispy, wispy, too perfect to pluck.

And the critters! Chipmunks, three together, Alvin-Simon-Theodore'd, a deer, at a distance, who sees and flees, squirrels, rabbits, a harmless snake, fingers crossed, turtles and frogs, ducks and geese, two swans, and some cardinals, orioles, and blue jays, play ball!

(No unicorns, ewoks, or tribbles?)

"And God saw all the things that he had made, and they were very good."
--GENESIS 1:31

I come to a footbridge spanning the river, but I do not cross, stopping mid-way to lean over the railing and look, the water below me now, fastly flowing, at lastly never, because as soon as, not. There's a straw hat surface swimming, a Frisbee floating, a soccer ball bobbing. I watch a plastic bottle slide-ride the current until it disappears downriver, taking some of me with it, because I'm no longer holding on tight, my cares and woes, I suppose, time slows, goes, no matter, no matter, sweet with independence, and possibility, and can't-remember-when-if-ever enough, because there's so much.

137

So…

I turn and return, flip side, untried, along the canal,
where once factories ferried, discerning fish therein,
black, assorted sizes, blinking up at me, misjudgingly, no
filet-o sandwiches I, or and-chips either, never, and
couldn't ever, now!

Some people that I passed going in the opposite direction
I pass going in the opposite direction, wink/wink, I
know, huh, something shared, been, both, and that's
definitely nice.

Eventually…

I finish where I started.

My Nike cellphone app has recorded 10,244 steps taken,
but God only knows how far I've gone!

In his essay "Walking," Henry David Thoreau notes that
the word "saunter" is thought to have been derived "from
idle people who roved about the country, in the Middle
Ages, and asked charity, under pretense of going *a la
Sainte Terre*, to the Holy Land."

As I sauntered along the Blackstone River, today, a
Sunday, early in the a.m., there was no idleness, no
pretense, and no going.

Holy land.

THE BLACKSTONE RIVER

At Lincoln, Rhode Island

WATCHING

(A One-Minute Meditation)

My husband David loves live web cams.

He watches cruise ships arriving and departing the Keys, pedestrians packing Times Square, and red trucks passing through Jackson, Wyoming.

He also watched a bird hatch an egg once.

"What's she doing? How long is it supposed to take? Where the hell is the father?"

The egg hatched after several weeks, but the chic lived only a few days.

David was heartbroken.

"It's so sad. Poor mother bird. Do you think she understands about life and death?"

And the cruise ships came and went, the people pulsed up and down Broadway, and the red trucks continued on.

COMPLEMENTAL VERSE

"THE SUN IS BUT A MORNING STAR,"
thus WALDEN ends,
my friends.
So let's awake to who we are,
intend, extend,
transcend!

FACT CHECK

"Do you mean to tell me...?"

My "interviews" are fake, but you understood that already, right? There is a thread of truth running through most of them, though. Thoreau did slaughter and devour that woodchuck, as you know only too well by now; he also helped his father improve pencil-making methods, tormented his seamstress, and put his jail cellmate through the third degree.

And Emerson wasn't really the sinister foil I've portrayed, either. Not 24/7, anyway. Some people actually liked him!

As for Jamblichus, Cato, and Tolstoy, well...

I've had tremendous fun writing this book.

I only wish I knew more about my subject!

("Why must biography be factually confined?")

If I've gotten anything wrong, my apologies. Please bring any errors to my attention, and I'll happily get all defensive.

Now let's go out there and front some onlys!

Tom

145

SOURCES

Works quoted, consulted, or referred to are as follows:

The writings of Henry David Thoreau, especially *Walden* (1854), "Sympathy" (1839), "On the Duty of Civil Disobedience" (1849), "Slavery in Massachusetts" (1854), "Life Without Principle" (1863), "A Plea for Captain John Brown" and "The Last Days of John Brown" (1860), "Walking" (1862), "Wild Apples" (1862), *A Week on the Concord and Merrimack Rivers* (1849), *The Maine Woods* (1864), and *Cape Cod* (1865).

The Writings of Henry David Thoreau. Edited by Bradford Torrey and Franklin B. Sanborn. Houghton, Mifflin. Copyright © 1906.

Poems of Nature by Henry David Thoreau. Edited by Henry S. Salt and Franklin B. Sanborn. Houghton Mifflin & Co. Copyright © 1895.

Familiar Letters by Henry David Thoreau. Edited by Franklin B. Sanborn. Houghton Mifflin & Co. Copyright © 1894.

Henry D. Thoreau by Franklin B. Sanborn. Revised edition. Houghton, Mifflin. Copyright © 1882.

The Days of Henry Thoreau: A Biography by Walter Harding. Originally published by Alfred A. Knopf, Inc., in 1965. Republished by Dover Publications, Inc., in 1982. Copyright © 1962, 1964, 1965, and 1982.

Henry David Thoreau: A Life by Laura Dassow Walls. University of Chicago Press. Copyright © 2017.

The People of Concord: One Year in the Flowering of New England by Paul Brooks. The Globe Pequot Press. Copyright © 1990.

The Portable Thoreau. Edited by Jeffrey S. Cramer. Penguin Classics. Updated ed. edition. Copyright © 2009.

The Night Thoreau Spent in Jail by Jerome Lawrence and Robert E. Lee. Hill and Wang, a division of Farrar, Straus and Giroux. Copyright © 1971, 1999, 2000.

Thoreau in Love by John Schuyler Bishop. CreateSpace Independent Publishing Platform. Copyright © 2013.

The writings of Ralph Waldo Emerson, especially "Nature" (1836), "The Over-Soul" (1841), "Self-Reliance" (1841), "The Transcendentalist" (1842), "Experience" (1844), and the Thoreau eulogy (1862).

The American Notebooks by Nathaniel Hawthorne. Ohio State University Press. Copyright © 1932, 1960, 1972.

"The New Colossus" by Emma Lazarus (1883).

The Douay-Rheims Bible. American Edition, 1899.

"What Do You Do with a B.A. in English?" Song from the musical *Avenue Q.* Music and lyrics by Robert Lopez and Jeff Marx. Copyright © 2004.

ACKNOWLEDGMENTS

I wish to thank the following for their help, support, and/or inspiration:

Erin Beasley and the National Portrait Gallery of the Smithsonian Institution.

The Library of Congress.

Ohio State University Press.

Depositphoto.com.

Amazon.com.

CreateSpace.com.

Kindle Direct Publishing.

BookDaily.com.

GoodReads.com.

Scott Hughes and OnLineBookClub.org.

Jack Magnus and ReadersFavorite.com.

Lionel Messi, Amos Lassen, Michelle Olms, Fran Soto, Len Evans Jr., Lynne Moody, Geri Novak, Michelle Stockard Miller, Stacia Chappell, Carol Teter Mauck, Ioana Simileanu, Micielle Carter, and Vermont Reviewer.

Professor Laura Dassow Walls, Ph.D.

Professor Brian M. Barbour, Ph.D.

Professor Clay V. Sink, Ph.D.

Marianne Wirth.

Bonnie at the Thoreau Farm.

The Walden Pond State Reservation.

The Walden Woods Project.

The Concord Museum.

The Concord Bookstore.

Susan at winstonflowers.com.

The Main Streets Market and Café.

The Thoreau-Alcott House.

The Morgan Library and Museum.

Debbie and the gang at Michaels craft store.

The Blackstone Valley State Park Visitors' Center.

And, of course, my husband David.

BY THE SAME AUTHOR

Ad Majorem
A Gay Man's Spiritual Testament

A story of faith, hope, and love which may inspire,
amuse, or offend, possibly all of the above.

5 OUT OF 5 STARS

"Well written, often humorous, and elegantly philosophical."

-- Readers' Favorite

If I'd a Knowed
A Gay Writer Writes About Writing and Other Stuff

A journey of self-discovery in self-publishing.

5 OUT OF 5 STARS

"Gifted.... Tom Beattie has a lot to say."

--Readers' Favorite

INTERVIEW WITH A CRITIC

"Tom Beattie"?

Yes, I've heard of him.

Unfortunately!

Let's just say he's no John Grisham, Anita Shreve, or J. K. Rowling.

His latest is a bio of Henry David Thoreau.

Fronting Onlys.

(Don't ask!)

But it's got woodchucks and girl scouts and gangsters...

Okaaay.

It's perfectly clear to me this book is a blind. To boost Thoreau's popularity, Emerson is maligned. That's a surefire recipe for a lawsuit and fines! Still, kudos to Beattie for his gay valentine. He may have an English degree, but--

Oh, never mind!

[Available for $6.73 in stores and online.]

Made in the USA
Lexington, KY
24 November 2017